WITHDRAWN

S0-BMY-474

THE MINISTER
BEHIND THE SCENES

By George Hedley

THE SYMBOL OF THE FAITH
A Study of the Apostles' Creed

THE CHRISTIAN HERITAGE IN AMERICA

THE SUPERSTITIONS OF THE IRRELIGIOUS

CHRISTIAN WORSHIP
Some Meanings and Means

RELIGION ON THE CAMPUS
Some Sermons in the Chapel of Mills College

THE MINISTER BEHIND THE SCENES

THE MINISTER
BEHIND THE SCENES

The James A. Gray Lectures
at Duke University, 1955

by

GEORGE HEDLEY

The Macmillan Company, New York, 1956

Carl A. Rudisill Library
LENOIR RHYNE COLLEGE

253.2
H 35m

© *The Macmillan Company 1956*

Published simultaneously in Canada

All rights reserved—no part of this book may be reproduced in any form without permission in writing from the publisher, except by a reviewer who wishes to quote brief passages in connection with a review written for inclusion in magazine or newspaper.

Printed in the United States of America

First Printing

33824
June, 1956

COPYRIGHT ACKNOWLEDGMENTS

Harcourt, Brace and Company, Inc., New York, and Faber and Faber, Ltd., London, for "Ash Wednesday" from COLLECTED POEMS 1909–1935, by T. S. Eliot, copyright, 1930 by T. S. Eliot and 1934, 1936, by Harcourt, Brace and Company, Inc.

Henry Holt and Company, Inc., for the poem "Mending Wall," by Robert Frost, copyright, 1930, by Henry Holt and Company, Inc., and 1936 by Robert Frost.

Random House, Inc., New York, and Faber and Faber, Ltd., London, "For the Time Being: A Christmas Oratorio," by W. H. Auden, Copyright, 1944, by W. H. Auden.

Library of Congress catalog card number: 56–7305

THE GRAY LECTURES

The James A. Gray Lectures are made possible through a fund presented to the Divinity School of Duke University in 1947 by Mr. James A. Gray, of Winston-Salem, North Carolina. In setting up this fund, the donor stated its general purpose to be "to extend and maintain the educational services of the Duke Divinity School in behalf of the North Carolina churches and pastors, particularly rural churches and pastors."

The first series of lectures on this foundation was delivered in 1950 by the Reverend Dr. Ralph W. Sockman, of Christ Church (Methodist), New York; the second in 1951 by the Reverend Professor Paul Ehrman Scherer, of Union Theological Seminary, New York; the third in 1952 by the Reverend Dr. Liston Pope, Dean of the Divinity School of Yale University; the fourth in 1953 by the Reverend Dr. Charles W. Gilkey, Dean of the Chapel and Professor Emeritus of Homiletics, of the University of Chicago; and the fifth in 1954 by the Reverend Dr. Henry Pitney Van Dusen, President of Union Theological Seminary, New York.

The present volume represents the sixth series of the Gray Lectures, delivered in 1955.

PREFACE

Through the years there have been made many books about the public activities and official responsibilities of the clergyman. It took the imagination of the Committee on the Gray Lectures to suggest an inquiry which should be limited strictly to the life and problems of "the minister behind the scenes." My first thanks go therefore to the members of that Committee, both for their nomination of the subject and for their invitation to me to discuss it. They are the Reverend Dr. James Cannon, Dean of the Divinity School of Duke University; the Reverend Dr. James T. Cleland, Dean of the University Chapel; and the Reverend Professors Robert E. Cushman, H. Shelton Smith, and Thomas A. Schafer, of the Divinity School faculty.

Next to be thanked is the Reverend Dr. Abbott Book, Executive Secretary of the Northern California–Nevada Council of Churches, who readily extended the use of the Council's facilities so that I might ask some typical ministers what they do with those hours when they are not before the public. Dr. Book's secretarial staff helpfully and cheerfully ran the addressograph. Thus I became involved in yet another debt of thankfulness, that to the 36 per cent of the addressees who took the trouble to complete and return the forms, and so allowed me to begin writing with evidence in hand. Especially do I incline my head toward—nay, I almost prostrate myself before —the reverend and anonymous gentleman who scrawled at the bottom of his copy, "This is the first questionnaire I have found worth filling out!"

During my week at Duke I found myself intensely grateful to President Arthur H. Edens of the University, and Mrs. Edens, and to Dean and Mrs. Cannon, for a hospitality that was no end impressive because it was in no way oppressive. As a sharer in the Christian Convocation of 1955, of which the lecture series was a part, I gained much from the public contributions and the personal courtesies of the Right Reverend Costen J. Harrell, Bishop of the Charlotte Area of the Methodist Church, who led the morning worship services, and of Dr. Cleland, who preached in the evenings. The singleness of our mood is illustrated in the fact that without prior consultation Bishop Harrell used in the Holy Communion, on Thursday, those prayers by William Bright and Cardinal Newman which already I had decided upon for the lecture hour on Friday, and which stand below with Lecture VI and the Epilogue.

There are many additional debts of gratitude. One is to the friendly, attentive, intelligently critical audiences at Duke. Another is to the household staff at University House, whose unobtrusive kindness restored to life an elder and gentler day than ours. Yet others are to some highly professional but wholly voluntary readers.

The original lecture drafts were read, and most helpfully criticized, by the Very Reverend James M. Malloch, Dean of St. James's Cathedral in Fresno, California, and by my two nearest (and almost dearest, but there are others as dear) clerical neighbors: the Reverend Donald G. Smiley, pastor of Laurel Methodist Church just west of the Mills College campus; and the Reverend Malcolm H. Miner, rector of St. Andrew's Episcopal Church, about the same distance southwestward.

The reading of the material about the minister's personal finances I inflicted on my former student the Reverend Dr. Roy E. Wilson, Executive Secretary of the Conference Claimants' Endowment Board of the California Conference of the Methodist Church. He contributed a lot of good sense to that section, but has no responsibility for any nonsense that may persist in it.

Grateful acknowledgments for permission to quote copyrighted materials are made to Mr. W. H. Auden, for nine lines from his "For the Time Being: A Christmas Oratorio"; to the Oxford University Press, for three lines from *The Testament of Beauty,* by Robert Bridges; to Messrs. Harcourt, Brace and Company, for five lines from T. S. Eliot's "Ash Wednesday"; to Mr. Robert Frost, for four lines from his "Mending Wall"; to Messrs. Harper and Brothers, for three lines from Aldous Huxley's "Orion"; and to George Allen and Unwin, Ltd., and the Oxford University Press for four lines from *Euripides,* translated by Gilbert Murray.

The time schedule at Duke University allowed for four lectures. To those I have added, in this more leisurely form, the "Lectures" now numbered III and V, and the section on "drama as reading" in Lecture II. Otherwise I have made few changes from the texts as delivered, and most of those in recognition of the simple factors of time and place.

Both in Durham and here in California, friends have asked why I failed to include discussions of pastoral calling, personal counseling, administrative procedures, and so on. The answer is that these belong to the area of the minister's public responsibility. So far as is possible, and admitting that there can be no absolute lines of demarcation, I have tried to limit these inquiries to the field which my good friends at Duke invited me to explore. We ministers, with all our public duty, spend a great deal of our time behind the scenes. I pray that these pages may help a little toward our spending it well.

GEORGE HEDLEY

Ruddigore, Mills College
St. James's Day, 1955

CONTENTS

CONTENTS

PROLOGUE

DIRECT us, O Lord, in all our doings, with thy most gracious favour, and further us with thy continual help; that in all our works begun, continued, and ended in thee, we may glorify thy holy Name, and finally, by thy mercy, obtain everlasting life; through Jesus Christ our Lord. Amen.
—Gregorian Sacramentary, A.D. 590.

*   *   *

The minister is a public person, and so of necessity he is an actor. Some observers have alleged that we parsons are mostly frustrated hams, showing off in the pulpit because we don't have what it takes to make good on the stage. However that may be, it is evident that a large proportion of the clergyman's time is spent in full view of the dual audience of his church and his community. Many are the rôles he is called upon to play: organizer, teacher, orator, executive, promoter, citizen, counselor, group worker, family man, friend, nowadays more and more often psychiatrist, though always he has had to be physician to sick and weary souls.

A professional actor does a maximum of eight two-and-a-half-hour shows a week. If he is an important member of the cast he may be actually on stage as much as one hour and thirty minutes each time. That adds up to twelve hours weekly. Occasionally the thespian meets the local press, and now and then for publicity's sake (or even for personal gratification) he may preen himself in the hotel lobby. Perhaps three additional hours a week are consumed by that sort of

1

thing. The rest of his time the matinee idol is hidden from public view, either relaxing or actively preparing himself for those brief periods out front.

It is not thus of the minister, for the parish ministry will not allow it to be thus. Rule out the pastor's family life if you will, because inevitably wife and children know him as he really is, and they are wholly unimpressed when he tries to put on an act for them. Rule out also any periods of public visibility but personal anonymity, for the world expects nothing in particular of those it doesn't happen to identify. There still remains a lot of time in the glare of the lights, whether the audience be a great throng on Sunday morning or a lone and troubled adolescent in the privacy of the study.

The peak of the clergyman's public responsibility may be the times of public worship, and they are relatively few: perhaps a total of three hours in the week. But there are also the Sunday school and the Young People's Fellowship; there are meetings of church boards and committees; there are the community gatherings in which a man has a growing part as he becomes a settled member of his neighborhood. There are dealings with secretary and janitor, with organist and choir director, with the officers of the Brotherhood and the women's society. That week will be rare which uses up less than six hours employed in such ways as these.

But that is not nearly all. The professional rôle has to be maintained unbrokenly, and no less by clergyman than by medico, alike in office visits and in house calls. A minister who really is serving his people finds his time increasingly demanded by those who need his services to them as individuals. At least five afternoons a week are likely thus to be claimed, or some fifteen to twenty hours more.

Finally, the minister must play the minister's part (in

2

whatever way he may conceive it) every time he steps out of the house in view of his neighbors. He is "Preacher" at the post office, "Doc" in the drugstore, "Reverend" to the grocery clerk. Somehow he has to establish in every contact both the dignity of his high calling and the warmth of his human interest, and not less with non-members of his parish than with those who are his special charge. There go two hours more of every day, certainly not less than ten on the weekly time budget.

All this adds up to some thirty-four to thirty-nine hours of treading the boards, with the curtain up and the lights ablaze. That is about what our modern age regards as a full week's work. The trick is that the really hard work, the essential work to make the ministerial stage appearances a success, has to be done backstage in the time that is left over.

A serious actor rehearses often, and a concert pianist practices several hours every day. How shall the minister discipline himself, how shall he prepare himself behind the scenes, so that adequately he shall play his part when the world can see him? This is the problem discussed in the pages that follow.

I

STUDYING THE PART
Professional Reading

The actor signed up for a new play is presented with a script which is a *fait accompli,* save for minor changes that may be made in rehearsals. Its total length is less than that of many a single book in the Bible, and of that length scarcely more than half at most is assigned to the individual player. Moreover the play is designed to be repeated many times, and with a minimum of alteration. A successful Broadway run, with a subsequent tour of the country, easily may mean unbroken repetition of exactly the same words and movements for the space of three full years.

By contrast the minister has no fixed script handed to him at all, except in so far as his church may have set forth a standard order for public services. Even in a ritual there are frequent variations and many options; and apart from the ritual there is unlimited room—and unlimited demand—for selection, arrangement, and invention. It is a dangerous practice for a preacher to indulge in much actual ad libbing in the pulpit; but his sermon scripts are, and inevitably have to be, prepared and calculated ad libs of the writing desk, unless he cribs them wholesale and without thought from other script men.

Getting up the ministerial part in advance, so that it

shall be done effectively when the curtain rises, is an infinitely harder and a much more independent job than is learning a theatrical rôle. Not for sermonizing only, but quite as much for unscheduled and sudden turns in conversation, the cleric has to be familiar with the words and meaning not of a hundred pages of dialogue, but of those countless pages of close printing which are the historic foundation of his assignment as herald of truth and curate of souls. To make matters still harder, the script boy is running in every few hours, whenever the mail may be delivered, with new materials from publishers and from denominational headquarters: materials which may or may not turn out to be relevant, but whose relevance can not be determined without the spending of precious time in their evaluation,

From a questionnaire filled out last autumn by clergy of thirteen different denominations, in northern California towns of under 40,000 population, I learned that the men estimate they spend an average of nineteen hours a week in reading. The highest figure reported was forty-eight hours, and the lowest four and a quarter. Frankly, I doubt the accuracy of both of the extreme statements; but I think the average estimate may be approximately accurate as to the average facts.

Breaking down this average total, one gathers that some six hours are devoted to what may be regarded as non-professional reading, or at least non-religious in the technical sense: fiction, secular non-fiction, poetry, secular magazines, and newspapers. That leaves thirteen hours of reading in the specifically religious field. The big items here for my California friends are the Bible, three hours and a half; current religious books, three hours and a quarter; and religious periodicals, two hours and a half. All in all, it would seem

5

that these gentlemen devote the equivalent of one and a half working days a week to the scripts that directly underlie their speaking parts.

The ticklish question, of course, is how they use this day and a half, and on what particular materials. That is the question for every one of us. What sort of professional reading shall we select for ourselves, and in what ratios among the various types? In what manner shall we do our reading, and with what specific ends in view?

Rediscovering the Bible

We all took Bible in the seminary. In retrospect, though, I wonder how much reading we actually did in the holy Scriptures themselves. We plowed through much of S. R. Driver, with the possible exception of some of the smaller print. (I say "smaller": in the edition I had, none of it was larger than "small.") We did about the same with E. F. Scott, though he was easier going both as to subject matter and in style. We bought the Hastings five-volume *Dictionary* from an importunate salesman, and occasionally we glanced through one of its articles for a quickie summary on a dubious point. Under pressure of term-paper assignments we even made a stab at a few volumes of the *International Critical Commentary*. We looked up particular verses for our sermon texts in Homiletics, and we may have checked a word or two of them in Greek or even in the Hebrew. I still ask whether we really took time to read the Bible at all; and I venture to ask also whether, now in our active ministry, we actually read the Bible or content ourselves with just reading about it.

One man among my northern Californians writes:

6

In my Baptist boyhood I read the entire Bible through four or five times to save my soul. I know it pretty well. But I do read the New Testament lesson in Greek every week.

That last is something: and if one goes through, and thinks through, fifty-two chapters of the original New Testament text every year, he is getting some real nourishment for his mind and soul. But as this ex-Baptist is now an Episcopalian, he presumably stays with the lectionary, and so is likely to be reading just about the same fifty-two chapters over and over again.

Nor does adult memory of boyhood reading, whether in a Baptist boyhood or not, provide any guarantee either of precise recall or of significant comprehension. It was thirty-two years ago that I first taught a college course in Bible, and I have been supposed to be able to teach Bible ever since. I have to confess that I don't know the Bible yet. The simple proof of this is that almost every time I look into it I find something I may or may not have seen before, but that certainly I never have registered before with any like intensity of appreciation and understanding.

Leafing through in hasty search for a Sunday-morning lesson, finding an apparently appropriate text with the aid of a concordance, looking again at Psalm 19 or St. John 1 or Romans 8: none of these is Bible reading in any significant sense. We read in order to discover and to learn. By reading introductions and dictionaries and commentaries we have learned much about the Bible, in our seminary days and perhaps even after them. The fact remains that in order to know the Bible we need to read the Bible itself; and this, I fear, is one of the things the busy pastor is the least likely to do.

Within these covers is the record and the evidence of

man's quest for God, and of God's self-revelation to man, over those twelve stirring centuries that gave foundation and form and furnishing to our great Hebrew-Christian tradition. Here are the first gropings and the ultimate insights, the bitter struggles and the triumphant realizings, the questions men must ask and the answers God alone can give. We shall apprehend the insights only as we share the gropings. We know not the triumph save as we experience the struggle. We understand the answers only after we have wrestled with the questions.

Two kinds of systematic approach may help. One is an approximation to the old "reading the Bible through"; but with the difference that the trained cleric does have some of the necessary footnotes already within his reach. He has learned in his Bib. Lit. classes that the J, E, D, and P documents of the Hexateuch originated centuries apart, and once upon a time he could reel off the lists of their distinguishing characteristics. Has he ever taken time, however, to trace through each of these documents as a consecutive unit, fully to taste its special savor and to absorb its particular points of view? Even if he has lost the copy he marked years ago with blue and red and green and brown Crayola, he can use E. S. Brightman as a guide; or even more easily he can follow in turn the plain type, the single square brackets, and the italicized sections, as they are marked off in the Moffatt version.

A chapter-by-chapter comparison of Samuel-Kings on the one hand, and Chronicles on the other, is scarcely less rewarding. What a world of difference there is between the early tales and their idealized rewriting; and how much we have in common both with the naïve narrator of King David's misadventures and with the revising institutionalist who set down instead what he wished might have happened! The characters in the tales, and the tellers of the tales no less, come alive for us as human individuals when we trouble to acquaint ourselves with them; and the more human they prove to be, the more we shall wonder and rejoice that God was able to speak to humankind through these thoroughly human voices.

In the New Testament our old friend "Q" is still worth following through, even if critically now we break "Q" up into a number of separate subcategories. The Gospel of St. Mark considered as a unit, perhaps in a Harmony so that the additions and modifications of St. Matthew and St. Luke may readily be noted, will give us a new sense of the exciting vitality of our Lord's mission among men. St. Paul as a case history in Christian maturation, both in thought and in spirit, comes marvelously clear when we take his authentic letters in their chronological rather than their conventional sequence. The change from the second Christian generation to the third, so important for us who look to the origins but live among the consequences, is strikingly exhibited when we lay Colossians beside its redoing in Ephesians, or the actual Paulines alongside the crystallized neo-Paulinism of I Timothy and Titus.

How long is it since we followed consecutively through the entire epistle to the Hebrews? Let's read it again, if we would understand at once the fallibility of our own churches and the saving grace of him who is able to keep us from falling. How often, since we were granted the two units of credit for the seminar in the Johannines, have we thought to enrich ourselves with the whole vision of the Word become flesh and dwelling among us? When last, with a world terror about us that makes A.D. 96 by comparison a piping time of peace, did we try really to feel with, dare with, believe with, the minority man of Patmos?

9

Along with our reading thus by authors, we shall profit also by reading the Scriptures again in terms of topics. Here the concordance and the Bible dictionary will help as starters, and so will the marginal references in our desk Bibles. Such aids are a menace, however, if they lead us but to single verses and encourage us to stop there. Some parts of the book of Proverbs are mere compilations of disparate fragments; but even in the wise men's pluralism there is more than we suspect of related and consecutive argument. For the rest of the Scriptures, subject matter is typically continuous, and single-sentence quoting is ever dangerous. It is well said that to use a text without reference to its context is to use it as a pretext; and that is no less true in private reading than it is in public sermonizing.

God is the Bible's primary subject. What, precisely, do the Biblical writers tell us God is like? The answer must be traced from the Jahvist's somewhat glorified man through Amos's annoyed supervisor of the nations to the second Isaiah's majestic planner of all history, and yet onward to the Synoptists' heavenly Father, and at the last to St. John's eternal Spirit of light and love.

What has the New Testament to say of Jesus Christ our Lord? St. Peter's speech on the day of Pentecost suggests divine adoption; St. Matthew's Gospel asserts Messiahship; St. Paul in Philippians speaks of a self-emptying; the Fourth Gospel declares the absolute glory made flesh. All these types of Christology are related, but they are not the same; and we shall know them for what they are only as we meet them, and meet them frequently, face to face.

Sometimes we shall be in for surprises. Last winter I was asked to preach a sermon about gambling. I could remember no Biblical treatment of the subject, and I had a wonderful time searching. It turned out that I searched in vain so far as a direct reply was concerned; but the datum that gambling seems not to have been a problem in Biblical times was in itself worth learning, and along the way I greatly refreshed my memory as to the casting of lots. Much more importantly, I came out with a new and enriched appreciation of the gospel of Christian carelessness, as expressed not only in the single text, "Be not anxious for the morrow," but also in the whole picture of Jesus' consistent and emphatic unconcern with things material.

Many questions of personal ethical behavior, reëxamined in the light of Scriptural judgments, may shift into a wholly new focus for us. There were certain Puritan clichés that long dominated American Protestantism, and more recently there have been liberal clichés scarcely less powerful and scarcely better scrutinized. What has our tradition actually to say about marriage? about the use of force and of violence? about self-denial and abstinence? about making money? about the relationship between religion and politics?

The Biblical thinking on these issues is more profound, more penetrating, and withal more perplexing, than our popular and unexamined assumptions have allowed us to suppose. We need to rethink all along the line. The first foundation for our rethinking is to discover how much thinking, how much hard and important and creative thinking, already is recorded in a series of books we quote more often than we peruse.

Early Christian Writings

We have come to the halfway point of this inquiry into the professional reading of the minister, and hitherto we have considered no books but those of holy Scripture. I will defend that proportion as a fully reasonable one. It is nevertheless true that one does not know the Bible if he knows the Bible only; and it is self-evident that eighteen hundred years after the closing of the canon we need to have some familiarity with what has occurred in these intervening centuries.

"Some Sunday," said a lady shaking hands after service, "will you tell us what happened between the death of Paul and the landing of the Pilgrim Fathers?" In her question, of course, she was betraying her own Congregational background. An Anglican would have fixed his nearer point at the compiling of the first *Book of Common Prayer,* and a Methodist at the Aldersgate Street experience of John Wesley. Here we Protestants all are pretty much alike, and therein equally unfortunate. We stop with the end of New Testament narration, and begin again only with the leader of our own particular segment of the Reformation: Luther, Calvin, Cranmer, Roger Williams, George Fox, Wesley, Alexander Campbell.

But a lot did happen in between, and much that we need to know if we are at all to understand how we became what we are now. Nor was George Park Fisher's one-volume *History* enough of an answer in my generation, nor is Williston Walker's in this. With all due respect to such careful and scholarly summarizers, one has to admit that Church History tasted exclusively in these unleavened and dehydrated wafers is a dull, flat diet indeed. It gains greatly in flavor, in saltiness if you will, the moment we make personal contact with the men who were making the history; and this contact we can secure only by reading what the men themselves wrote.

Forty-four per cent of my California clergy friends indicate that they devote no time at all to the reading of early

Christian literature other than the New Testament. Think of what thereby they are missing of acquaintance with original and heroic spirits, and of light on the critically important determining of doctrine and organization, in the time just after the earliest generation of Christian leaders had left the earthly scene. Let us transport ourselves now to those years following immediately upon the deaths of Saints Peter and Paul.

We find that St. Clement of Rome, in A.D. 96, still is wrestling with the forty-year-old problem of internal disputes in the church at Corinth. St. Ignatius of Antioch, being taken under military guard to his execution in the imperial capital, pauses on the way to send "heartiest greetings of pure joy" to the Christians of Ephesus, and takes time to warn them against false teachers in their midst. St. Justin, a Greek philosopher by training, uses the categories of Greek philosophy to defend a sturdy, simple Christian faith. The usages and procedures of a second century parish are clearly outlined both in his essays and in the contemporary manual known as "The Teaching of the Twelve Apostles."

A generation later St. Irenaeus, transplanted from his native Asia Minor to a bishopric at Lyons in Gaul, argues for a central Christian authority in order to guard the central Christian position against the vagaries of new sects that are multiplying on the fringes. (Oh, what a happy warrior Irenaeus would be if he had a charge in Los Angeles today!) Clement of Alexandria carries forward the argument of St. Justin, and in the process turns ever more of Greek thinking to Christian uses. Tertullian, a North African lawyer, writes enthusiastically and voluminously in support of views so uncompromising that at last the Church itself concludes it must disown him. St. Hippolytus of Rome does his best to organize both Christian doctrine and ecclesiastical practice into coherent patterns.

Limits of space forbid the mention, by more than name, of such as St. Polycarp and Athenagoras, and Origen and St. Cyprian, and the many pseudonymous authors of new Gospels and Acts and Revelations. All of these are well worth knowing in their own right, and each of them has something special to tell us of how real were the issues that arose, and how ingenious and brave (and miscellaneous) the solutions that were devised, in the formative days of the Church in the second and third Christian centuries. These ministers of old time ought to be our friends, for their experiences and their difficulties were much like our own. They well may be our guides and our inspiration, for they found many a viable if now forgotten answer to the questions that we, their successors, are asking from day to day.

Yet another century begins, and again the problems of that distant past are those of 1955. Do our young people confront us with naïve but fearfully puzzling questions about the nature of the Holy Trinity? We shall handle them the more confidently, and the more accurately, in so far as we know how the Church wrestled with this mystery in the fourth century and after. If we know this, moreover, we shall drop the silly nonsense of saying that there was no important difference between "same essence" and "similar essence."

Are we confused as to where we stand, and ought to stand, about the relations of church and state? There is scarcely a better place to begin the analysis than with St. Augustine's *City of God*. (I do not discount his much more widely used *Confessions;* but these reflect only one facet of the many-sided bishop's mind, and not the most original nor the most strikingly significant for our present world scene.)

Again we must skip down the years, though our reading and our knowledge ought not to skip in any such way. Pause to note St. John Chrysostom's liturgy, though, and St. Gregory Nazianzen's repudiation of the heresies that denied alternatively our Lord's Godhood or his true humanity, and St. Gregory's homilies to his Roman parishioners, and Alcuin's revision of Gregory's manual of prayers, and St. Anselm's profound answer to the question, "Why a God-man?" Let Duns Scotus awake the somnolent mind, and Abélard force it into violent exercise. Let St. Thomas Aquinas amaze and baffle those of us who have thought that theological questions permit of any easy answers. This faith of ours inquires into all that is and all that ought to be. We do the faith scant service if we fail to pursue the inquiry for ourselves, with all the intellectual power that we have and with every aid that we can find. Such aid is abounding among those fathers of the Church who through the ages pioneered the chasms of question and the summits of reply.

Protestant Beginnings

It is tempting to suppose that Protestants, blind as many of them have been to the values and contributions of the one Church that existed before our dividings, know at least the founders of their own respective movements. I wonder whether this is as true as we would like to claim. Does the modern Lutheran read the treatises of Martin Luther? How often does today's Presbyterian open a copy of John Calvin's *Institutes?* How much of John Wesley's work, aside from Bishop Herbert Welch's well chosen but minimal sampling in the *Selected Writings,* is familiar to the Methodist?

The difficulty is that which we have noted in the case of

the Bible: that commonly, instead of reading the original sources, we merely read about them. The hero of a given tradition thus quickly becomes a myth, cast in the likenesses of his various biographers, and therefore one whose resemblance to the historic figure is more or less coincidental. He who reads the authentic Luther will learn that he can no longer regard the hero of Wittenberg and Worms as a bulwark for the slavish Biblical literalism in which so many of his professed followers have entrapped themselves. He who examines the actual Calvin will find far more of flexibility in that flinty character than survived in the patterns of the Auld Kirk. He who lives a while with the real Wesley may wonder, now and then, what Wesley would think of the sloppiness in worship, and the noisiness of utterance, which many Americans take to be the inevitable marks of Methodist enthusiasm.

It is conceivable that, when we come to know these heroes of our several Protestant legends as they really were, some of us will be disappointed in them. An American Presbyterian edition of the *Institutes of the Christian Religion,* published in Philadelphia in 1833, devoted much of its preface to lamenting Calvin's error in denying that the Jewish Sabbath regulations applied at all to the Christian Sunday. A Methodist may honestly dissent from Wesley's view that every devout believer should receive the Holy Communion at least once a week. (For the record, let me make it clear that I personally find myself in agreement with the sacramentarian Mr. Wesley.) A Disciple may cling to the "King James" version of the Scriptures as a verbally inspired document, in despite of Alexander Campbell's judgment that it was already inadequate in 1826. We are by no means required to accept the men of former days as dictators of our present thinking. But neither are we permitted to cite them as authority for our positions unless they held those positions; and we shall have to read their writings if we are to know just where they did stand.

Let me recommend here one particular series of volumes which is now in process of issue. It is "The Library of Christian Classics," being published in Britain by the Student Christian Movement and in this country by the Westminster Press. There will be twenty-six volumes all told, of which eleven are now available. The beginning is with St. Clement of Rome, and the end will be a compilation from the works of the English reformers. Three volumes are devoted to St. Augustine, four to Luther, and four to Calvin. This is by no means an exhaustive compendium, but it is a thoughtfully selected and carefully edited anthology; and it is a minimum of what the minister needs to be at home with if he is to apprehend the Christian tradition in its historic unfolding from the first century to the sixteenth.

Current Religious Writing

Still the newly written books pour from the presses, and still curiosity and clerical conversations drive us to do some reading in these too. The problem here is manifestly one of selection. How shall we decide, in advance of reading, which of the myriad candidates for our attention are worth expending of our time, our money, and our effort?

Of the California clergy who responded to my queries, 44 per cent belong to one or more of the several book clubs in the religious publishing field, and another 14 per cent have belonged at one time or another. One chap put a very emphatic exclamation point after his "No!" to the book-club question. No doubt what troubled him was the problem of point of view. The choices of any book club reflect the assumptions of its own corps of judges as to what sort of work exhibits sound thinking and provides helpful statement. There will be a kind of sameness, therefore, in the selections of any one club from year to year. This is not in itself bad, if the central position itself be a sound one; but it does suggest that a book club scarcely can provide the total answer for a genuinely inquiring mind.

Reviews in the religious press (including, of course, those in the book-club bulletins themselves) offer more variety and a fair amount of accurate information. Again, however, there is danger of imprisonment within a single pattern if one accepts the guidance of one journal only, or of one closely related group of journals. There can be scarcely an author anywhere who has not had one and the same book of his praised for clarity by one reviewer, and damned for opacity by another, or hailed in one sheet as revolutionary illumination and assailed in a second as a piece of traditionalist obscurantism. Reviewers are worth paying attention to, unless (as the custom of some is) they merely copy out the publisher's jacket blurb. But no reviewer is right all of the time, and every reviewer needs checking by comparison with his colleagues, and especially with his opponents.

There are choices also that we shall have to make about subject matter. I have challenged our tendency to read secondary material about the Bible while failing to read the Bible itself. This ought we to have done, yet not to have left the other undone. Much keeps on happening in Biblical scholarship, and for many of us older men a tremendous lot has happened since we left the divinity school. How well have we been keeping up?

An immediate and important aid here is *The Interpreter's Bible,* now two-thirds of the way to completion. I have formed the habit of reading at once, as each successive

volume has come to hand, the introductions to the several
Biblical books. Much that is in them is familiar to anyone
who has worked in the field in this century. A varying
amount is new to any given reader, and in some cases a
great deal. For today, and for a reasonable number of years
to come (though certainly not for ever), this *magnum opus*
of the Methodist press is the best single summary of the
state of informed opinion about Biblical authorships, historical settings, and essential meanings. I do not hesitate to
say that it is required reading for every man who presumes
to speak with knowledge of the Scriptures as a product of
man's contact with God in history.

Theology is no more static than is Biblical criticism, and
the minister is obligated to keep up with what goes on in
theological thinking and discussion. Many of us now in
active service had our training in the heyday of liberal
modernism, and too many of us stopped thinking at that
point; which means that we now are guilty of the same
stubborn reluctance to learn which we used to charge
against those "hidebound mossbacks" who were senior
to us.

Maybe neo-orthodoxy isn't the total or final answer. I
don't think it is for me. But it certainly is the vital and
uncompromising challenger today of what we were taught
to think yesterday; and we are ignorant of the Christianity
of 1955 until we have come to grips with Barth and Brunner
and Niebuhr and Tillich. —Yes, they will drive us back
inevitably to Kierkegaard, and thither too we must go in
our compulsory quest for meaning. It is, I think, too early
yet to know whether we shall be going forward if we follow
the lead of the "neo-liberalism" that now is being promul-
gated from the Federated Theological Faculty in Chicago.
Nevertheless we shall need to read these reinterpretations

also, if we propose to engage in illumined interpreting on our own account.

Along with the revival of profound theological concern, there has been in our time a reawakening of interest in the meaning and means of Christian worship. No longer is the church regarded, as so long it was in the American Protestant scene, as being primarily an auditorium for the hearing of sermons. At long last we are returning to where John Wesley always was: to the conviction that not the speaking of man, but the worshiping of God, is the primary purpose of the assembling of Christians together.

Yet we have been so long separated from this realization that we are rusty, and we need a good deal of polishing up. Worship materials, and books about the history and the methodology of public worship, are appearing in increasing number. These also we need to read, mark, learn, and inwardly digest, that we may qualify ourselves worthily to lead our people in worthy declaring of the worth-ship of our everliving God, in meaningful commitment of our whole selves to the joy of his salvation and the doing of his will.

A newer field than these in terminology and technique, though an infinitely old one in basic fact, is that of pastoral counseling. It is a revealing datum that the Pastoral Psychology Book Club stands second only to the original Religious Book Club in popularity among my California pastors. Today the seminaries are doing much in this area: so much that some of us who are traditionalists are wondering whether Biblical and theological scholarship may in some cases be going to the wall. For those of us who have been out of school for a generation, however, the shoe is on the other foot.

No one in my seminary ever told me that at age twenty-three I would be expected to be a father confessor to a whole New England township, and certainly no one offered any hint as to how I should go about the job. By this time most of us have found *ad hoc* answers with which we get along fairly well; but all of us would profit by a better acquaintance with the inner nature of psychological stresses, and with the now standard professional procedures that have been worked out to deal with them. My own opinion is that there is a fairly early point of diminishing returns in this area, and always I would count personal experience the most important single guide. Nevertheless we as counselors need all the help that we can get; and we ought to know at least what kind of help is available to us in the literature of pastoral care.

Religious Periodicals

Those California padres subscribe for an average of five periodicals per man (the range being from none to ten), of which the religious ones dominate in the ratio of exactly two to one. Almost every man takes at least two of his own denominational papers, and more than 25 per cent are readers of the *Christian Century*. It is fascinating to note, incidentally, that nearly half the readers of the *Christian Advocate*, in this sampling, are ministers of churches other than Methodist.

What is the religious journal's function? Some of them are merely house organs, keeping one in touch with who's moving where and what's going on in those parishes that happen to have active publicity committees. These are interesting to those who know the people and the places, but they are scarcely of first importance to anyone. Others of our publications may be described as trade sheets, dealing chiefly with professional and technical procedures. They are useful within their limits, but those limits are narrow ones. Finally there are the journals of research and opinion, whose function is to supplement the serious books and to keep us in continuous touch with the living currents of religious thinking.

Surely it is this last category that is worth the most. Am I taking too dim a view when I register my suspicion that it is the one that is read the least? Not promotion, but religion, is the primary concern of the ministers of God. We get the *Pastor's Journal* or its equivalent willy-nilly, and we learn some useful and necessary things from it. We have to take initiative, and to spend a little money (unless there's a good library handy), to get at *Religion in Life*. There are treasures to be found here too, and richer ones than a house organ is designed to supply. I am not proclaiming an either/or. In all solemnity I do plead for a both/and.

Has all this been a counsel of perfection, impossible to follow in the pastor's busy life? Of course it's not easy. Few things worth doing are. Yet my Californians say they give twelve or more hours a week to religious reading. If truly it is religious reading, and not just desultory reading in the religious field, it should provide room for much that really counts.

Twelve hours a week? Why not budget them then, consciously and mathematically? Four hours weekly to rediscover God's word in his holy Scriptures: who would want to spend less? Four hours in each seven days to locate ourselves in the magnificent but intricate history of Christian faith and order through the ages: who can know the life and teaching of the Church without at least that much time spent in earnest and persisting inquiry? There still are four hours left for the newer works: books on the Bible, on theology, on worship, on counseling. Serious journals well may be fitted into that time; the lighter ones can be disposed of in the lulls before and after supper. Twelve hours: how much we can do with them, how much we can grow in them, if only we will.

Never more than today has it been essential that every man of God should be throughly furnished unto all good works. Not only the Scriptures of old, but the God-seeking and God-finding books of every age, are critically important factors in that furnishing. The rôle which has been assigned to us is that of the workman approved unto God, rightly dividing the word of truth. If we are to master the part, we shall have to remember and obey the first word of the long-ago injunction to the young pastor Timothy. We all know what it was: "Study!"

*   *   *

BLESSED Lord, who hast caused all holy Scriptures to be written for our learning; grant that we may in such wise hear them, read, mark, learn, and inwardly digest them, that by patience and comfort of thy holy word, we may embrace, and ever hold fast, the blessed hope of everlasting life, which thou hast given us in our Saviour Jesus Christ. Amen.
—Book of Common Prayer, A.D. 1549.

II

KNOWING THE STAGE

Collateral Reading

ALMIGHTY God, unto whom all hearts are open, all desires known, and from whom no secrets are hid; cleanse the thoughts of our hearts by the inspiration of thy Holy Spirit, that we may perfectly love thee, and worthily magnify thy holy Name; through Christ our Lord. Amen.
            —Sacramentary of Alcuin, about A.D. 800.

*   *   *

The subject which the committee at Duke University originally suggested for the second of the Gray lectures, to follow the opening inquiry into "professional reading," was set down as "desultory reading." I took leave to register a mild objection, on the ground that none of us had time to spend in discussion of anything so inconsequential. Assuming that the intent was to call attention to a minister's reading outside his professional and technical field, I suggested that what we had to deal with was the kind of reading which is called "collateral."

As I remember the "collateral reading" in History courses in my undergraduate days, it was not regarded as incidental, and certainly it was not expected to be desultory. We had to hand in not only lists showing chapters and/or page numbers, but also outlines establishing that we had some personal knowledge of the sections listed. My better teachers took it for granted that a good deal

24

of reading outside the primary textbook was integral to grasp of the field; and with such instructors that student fared ill who had not enriched his center of learning by drawing upon the circumference.

This is precisely the situation for the minister who wants to be equal to his assignments. Not only does he need familiarity with the Bible and theology and worship and counseling. He is set in a total community, and his church exists in a total world. Nothing human then may he consider alien to himself, and no field of knowledge is irrelevant to the full equipping of the servant of God. His specific part is religious, Biblical, theological. The stage on which he plays that part is political, social, economic, cultural. Only if he knows his stage thoroughly is he qualified to move freely about its spaces, and to enact upon it his required rôles as leader of thought, strengthener of spirit, and inspirer of action.

Let us take our departure again from the California clergymen's reports on their own practice. Six hours and a half, they say, are devoted each week to reading outside the specifically religious field. The breakdown shows an average of two hours and a quarter for daily newspapers, two hours for secular non-fiction books, one hour and a quarter for secular magazines, three-quarters of an hour for current fiction, and, finally, a quarter of an hour for poetry.

Only 8 per cent of these men belong to any book club other than the religious ones, but there are fully half as many subscriptions to secular as to religious periodicals. The typical ministerial library, of some five hundred volumes, runs an average of 29 per cent secular books to 71 per cent religious. Forty-nine per cent of the men indicate that they make little use of the local public library; 43

per cent depend on it a lot; and the remaining 8 per cent are equivocal on this point.

Newspapers and Magazines

Several years ago, when our Mills College seniors in Sociology and Economics were talking over their impending comprehensive examinations, I ventured to suggest some questions that I thought might be typical. One girl looked horror-stricken. "Why," she protested, "that means we'd have to read the newspapers!" I apologized to her then, and I have felt apologetic ever since, for our department's abject failure in its attempts to educate her. How she got to be a senior with us without reading the daily papers I never shall know. At all events, she had a thorough workout on them in the one semester that remained of her college life.

A minister need not be a major in "Soc-Econ," and he certainly ought not to be so far as the principal subjects of his thinking, teaching, and preaching are concerned. But no one who hopes to exercise any sort of leadership today can afford not to read the daily press. Six per cent of the Californians record for themselves no newspaper reading at all, though one of these provides something of a balance by subscribing for the *Atlantic Monthly,* the *Saturday Review,* and the *New Yorker.*

There were two happy periods in my life, each of them of several months' duration, when I didn't see a newspaper at all. I confess that I felt something of relief therein, and that I was just a little reluctant to return to the modern world from the caves and the potsherds of five thousand years ago. Yet I did have to return; and there is no escape from the papers for those who are living in the atomic age instead of in the Aëneolithic.

Yes, much that is in the newspapers is troubling, disheartening, infuriating. That is a principal reason why the Christian minister must pay attention to it. Christianity is a real religion, and a realistic one. True Christianity blinks neither the fact of original sin, nor the facts of mankind's current and highly versatile sinning. The saving gospel is for sinners; and when it offers them salvation, it does so meaningfully only as it reckons with the particular kinds of sin in which these particular sinners have got themselves involved.

Would we build a world of love? We need then to analyze the structures of hatred. Do we look forward to the establishing of peace among men? We must be familiar first with the sources and the techniques of conflict. Is our goal the kingdom of God upon the earth? We shall gain it only if our espionage service reveals accurately the secrets of the kingdom of the devil. That there is so much of the devilish reported in the press, so much of conflict, so much of hate, makes the daily paper often sad reading; and by the same token it makes it required reading for every one of us.

Two protests often are heard: (*a*) that the press is inaccurate in its reporting; and (*b*) that it is biased in its editorializing. Both these charges are to some extent true, but neither excuses us from the obligation to read nevertheless. Errors of fact, I seriously believe, spring less often from deliberate intent than from the reporters' haste and from their lack of background knowledge in specialized fields. We shall just have to grit our teeth when we find mistaken or misleading statements (even as we do when the paper uses such popular barbarisms as "Reverend Jones"), and proceed by every means we can to set the record straight.

As a party Democrat, I find myself regularly and richly annoyed by many of the political editorials in our Oakland and San Francisco dailies, which without exception are Republican. As a sociologist, I alternately cringe and squawk when a paper comes forth with what seems to me to be ponderous idiocies about how to deal with juvenile delinquency or drug addiction or unconventional opinion on a college campus. The more annoyed I am, the more I know I must plow through the annoying stuff, because I must discover as accurately as I can just what sort of public opinion the editorial pages are trying to mold, and by precisely what means.

Our people in the churches, being members of the community at large, inevitably are much influenced by those prevailing tides of sentiment that the newspapers at once reflect and seek to create. We may not hope to bring our congregations toward what we believe they should be unless we meet them where they are. If we are to meet them there, we shall have to be familiar with all that has conditioned their thinking, their emotions, and their prejudices. The less we happen to approve, the more requisite it is that we shall thoroughly comprehend.

The newspaper will supply us with the facts of current history, at least with something like accuracy. Nor do I exclude the possibility that sometimes, and through some of its writers, it may provide also useful stimulus, and even constructive guidance, for our own thinking. Greater factual precision, however, and considerably less prejudicial treatment, will in the nature of the case be found in the more leisurely and less excited pages of the major monthly magazines. A subscription to *Harper's* or the *Atlantic,* for example, will provide an overview of the present scene that no daily or even weekly summary of raw events can possibly achieve. Failing a subscription, an occasional but recurring hour in the public library with one of these will do much to keep us in touch with what the better informed men and women of our country know, and with what the better trained minds in our society are thinking.

Current Non-Fiction

Still more stable than the monthly journals, because still more leisurely and relaxed, are the serious books of non-fiction. Their scope is wider too, for they are not limited to the immediate episodes and issues of today. Much has been reëxamined in the story of mankind since we were in school, and much has been significantly rewritten. Not all of us can get at any large amount of source material in the historical field, but all of us can learn to identify the historians who use the sources with insight and integrity.

For a single example, take the work of the late Douglas Southall Freeman. No doubt an audience in North Carolina knew a lot more than a Californian did about Lee and his generals; but it learned still more when Freeman wrote of them. And how livingly real, how humanly noble, an earlier Virginia gentleman became for all of us as Freeman put together the fruits of his research about George Washington. We all are better Americans, and therein we are better qualified to be Christians in America, for experience with works such as these.

There are adventurings in distance as well as in time. From Greenland to Patagonia, from the Philippines to Morocco, from Denmark to Pakistan, man has journeyed, observed, and recorded. Not all of God's children are exactly like us. If we and they are to live constructively and creatively in God's present world of multiplying numbers and diminishing miles, we need that closer acquaintance which will interpret our differences in terms of considered appreciation rather than in those of automatic opposition.

This last February I read (and it took me late evening after late evening in February to do it, for it is a big book) E. Lucas Bridges' *Uttermost Part of the Earth*. This is the autobiography of an English boy born and brought up in Tierra del Fuego, among one of the most primitive groups of people in the world. He lived in their midst all of his more than eighty years; he knew them thoroughly; he loved them completely; and he wrote of them simply and brilliantly. It was good to meet so gallant a gentleman in the pages of his book; and it was good to meet and to know the fur-clad, blubber-eating Firelanders as authentic ladies and gentlemen too.

Then there is adventure for its own sake. Someone recently remarked that the sure way to do a best-seller is almost to climb a mountain, and then to write a detailed account of the failure. The "almost" doesn't matter one way or the other, if the climbing itself was well and bravely done. Everest, Annapurna, K2, Makalu, Kanchenjunga: what visions of daring, what miracles of self-giving, they evoke! I have a colleague who assigns to his classes in the religion of India the reading of the mountain literature; for he believes (and I think rightly) that the Himalayas of granite and ice provide some of the best of commentaries on the Himalayas of the spirit, the rugged peaks that man must climb if indeed he would come near to God.

Earlier, as a schoolboy, I fed my own soul on Ernest

Shackleton and Robert Falcon Scott, and I own an un-
dying gratitude to those courtesy uncles who put their
stories into my hands. Shackleton's ship *Endurance* was
sunk in the Weddell Sea, without ever touching the Ant-
arctic Continent: but if you would know how far man
can go to win the spirit's victory over things material, read
again in *South* how that brave captain brought all his ex-
pedition out alive. Scott and his polar party didn't even
come out alive; but the memory of that lonely tent in the
blizzard on the Ross Shelf Ice lives evermore to attest the
magnificence that can belong to humankind. More recently,
and without the tragic ending, there is the story of Admiral
Byrd's lonely and heroic vigil in the emptiness between
the Bay of Whales and the Liv Glacier, and of what he
learned for his own spirit in that wintry solitude.

Back now to the nearer and the more prosaic, though not
to the less difficult and challenging. Two years ago I guest-
taught, at a well known school of theology, a course in
"Christianity and Industrial Relations." Checking the
school's library, I learned to my horror that it didn't include a single book on labor relations that had been written
since World War I; and I had to take over an automobile
load of items from my own shelves, only to begin to give
the men a chance at some of the facts of today. The economics and sociology of our daily life are fearfully complicated,
and they need the Economics and Sociology of our most
competent scholars to bring them for us into any framework of sense.

It is not enough for the minister, living in a mill town,
to take his ideas about management and unions from the
daily press, or from occasional items in *Time* or the *Reader's
Digest*. Neither can he learn all he ought to know merely
by observation and conversation on the spot, for his data

gained thereby scarcely will be complete and almost certainly will be inaccurate at some crucial points. He needs a background and systematic understanding of the problems of wages, of unemployment, of collective bargaining, of the social psychology of the inevitable competition between owners and workers in the distributing of industry's money product. Such orderly, informed, and reasoned interpretation is in his reach. He must learn to use it, rather than to depend on expressions of thoughtless bias against labor on the one hand, and of sentimental sympathy with the downtrodden workingman on the other. This is essential if he is to know what goes on, and so is to be of some use in meeting the stresses of an industrial community.

Exactly the same is true for those whose ministry is chiefly to farmers. We city folk take a dim view of having to pay government-rigged prices for our food. They whose parishioners are rural hear much complaint over the way the city juggles things to the farmer's disadvantage. No one of us is qualified to discuss these issues intelligently, let alone to help to deal with them constructively, without having read and digested a few objective and dispassionate studies of this complex and controversial field of agricultural economics.

A fortiori, the general economic scene requires our careful and penetrating attention, for we have to play our parts upon the whole of the daily shifting economic stage. Some of us remember our college Econ. 1 as a tour de force in mathematics and graphs, without ever a hint that it had the slightest relationship to our own future income and expenditure. The economists have learned a lot about reality in these subsequent decades of depression and inflation, and they have recorded accurately and interpreted honestly.

32

No good book on economics can be easy, but all the really good ones make sense to anyone who has sense enough to care about the problem. By way of a single recommendation, I suggest looking into the symposium called *Twentieth Century Economic Thought,* edited by my longtime colleague at Mills College, Professor Glenn E. Hoover, and published in 1950. I dare anyone to read that, and then ever again to mutter the hoary lie that college economists don't understand the facts of business life. We of the cloth would be a lot better off than we are, as to comprehension and perhaps even as to cash, if we understood them half as well.

Studies of Man and Society

The more we read the serious writings of today, the more we shall realize how deeply rooted they are in what was thought and written many years, even many centuries and millennia, ago. I used to offer, on the University of California Extension Division, a one-semester one-unit survey called "Studies of Man and Society." We devoted two class hours each to the examining of eight major works, every one of which seems to me to be of permanent and critical importance in our attempts to deal with yesterday, today, and tomorrow.

We began with Plato's *Republic,* as one of the first and most meaningful attempts to determine how man might achieve a social order of intelligent justice. I would add here at least Plato's *Phaedo,* an application of the same principles to those choices that have to be made in every individual's life; and the *Ethics* and *Politics* of Aristotle as well—harder going, these, but the very foundation of Western social and political thinking ever since.

33

Then we turned to St. Augustine's *City of God*. This historic study of history was written over a period of fourteen years while the empire of Rome was collapsing before barbarian assault, even as our own civilization seems to be. It is well to ask ourselves again, with the fifth century Bishop of Hippo, what enduring values may survive the wreckage of a single and familiar culture pattern.

No city of God was it that Machiavelli wrote of in *The Prince,* but it has been many a city of man. The Florentine civil servant was a mordant pragmatist, though by no means so unprincipled as non-reading repute has made him. There is no more revealing introduction to the study of actual political behavior, as distinct from constitutional and statutory formulae, than this picture of empirical statecraft in that emerging Renaissance whose closing days now are upon us.

In furious intellectual rebellion against the Renaissance state, and as a precursor of social and political revolution in France, there arose Jean-Jacques Rousseau. This scapegrace music copyist was an incorrigible romantic, whose "noble savage" was a figment of imagination quite uncomplicated by anthropological fact, and whose principles of education he never ventured to try on his own children. He was yeast nevertheless to the political ferment of Europe, and as notably to the educational theories that were to be put into polysyllabic prose at Teachers College more than a century later. *Émile* and *The Social Contract* stand therefore on the primary shelf for him who would understand the new departures in school and state in the past two hundred years.

An incisive analyst of man's problems even less accurately portrayed in popular supposition than Machiavelli has been, was the prince of all economists, Adam Smith.

Whether one is a sturdy defender of private enterprise, or an eager young radical devoted to the building of the welfare state, he is permitted neither to adore Adam Smith, nor to execrate him, till he has read what the eighteenth century Scot had to say. One who does read *The Wealth of Nations* will find that it is not at all what its more vocal applauders and its most vociferous detractors have united in trying to make it.

The Glasgow Professor of Moral Philosophy believed in freedom indeed, but in real freedom. No supporter of tariffs and subsidies, of quotas and "fair trading," will find any comfort in this man's smashing attacks upon all the devices that commerce has used in the restraint of trade. Humanity's wealth, Smith maintained, consists not in the possession of gold but in the production of goods; and that production, he held, is not aided but stifled by the self-seeking of anyone (repeat, *anyone*) who tries to use government as an instrument in the protection and promotion of his private interest.

Not less upsetting to deep-rooted social tradition was Charles Darwin's work in *The Origin of Species* and *The Descent of Man*. Again the classic documents need to be examined in their own right, as a defense against all the nonsense that both believers and unbelievers have talked about the evolutionary hypothesis. Darwin's work indeed was not final, and no scientist's ever can be. It was nevertheless the critical contribution, the one which forced the world to remake not only its biological theories but also its philosophical assumptions.

Let us get it into the record, too, that Darwin, who was trained at Cambridge for the Church, was no atheist. One quote, of the very last sentence in *The Origin of Species*, is enough to give pause to any who faithlessly suppose that

evolutionary development is beyond the power of the om-
nipotent God. "There is grandeur in this view of life," our
author concludes after nearly four hundred pages of his
careful, systematic piling up of detailed evidence,

with its several powers, having been originally breathed by
the Creator into a few forms or into one; and that, whilst this
planet has gone cycling on according to the fixed law of gravity,
from so simple a beginning endless forms most beautiful and
most wonderful have been, and are being evolved.

We tackled Karl Marx too in that extension class, and
found ourselves not converted to Communism. What a
quaint and cowardly notion it is that the politico-economic
heresy of Marx and his followers is so potent that any ex-
posure to it is certain to mean conquest by it. We need to
know what Marx did think, and what his followers real and
alleged are thinking, if we are to be halfway conscious of
what goes on in half the world today. Our class consensus
was that Marx's writing is its own strongest confutation,
especially when its labored and turgid rationalizings are
seen beside the clear, inescapable reasonings of Adam
Smith. *Das Kapital* bores even its defenders; but here is a
case in which boredom has to be endured by all who claim
title to an opinion about the system which most of us prefer
to hate without having seen.

Last of all in this course sequence we looked at Oswald
Spengler in *The Decline of the West*. Here is another typical German treatise, overloaded with erudition and wandering through endless mazes of technical detail. Yet the thesis
Spengler advanced in 1918, that our Western culture and
civilization are slipping downhill to their inevitable doom,
is even harder to refute in 1955 than it was when our age's
greatest pessimist first enunciated it. Perhaps our way of

living can be saved for posterity. I pray, and I soberly believe, that it can. But it never will be saved by those who refuse to diagnose its maladies. Of all men the Christian minister should care most about the preserving of the freedom that has made us free; and so he needs more than all others to recognize the threatening symptoms of bondage, that he may contend effectively againt the Caesar in the cause of the Christ.

Current Fiction

Another kind of interpretation of the current human scene is afforded by the serious fiction of our day. Of this there is so much that no one but the professional reviewer of novels can hope to keep up with all. Yet none but the refugee from living facts and from the thought currents of our time may venture to avoid the modern novelist altogether.

My own experience was a fortunate one. I had an intensive spell of fiction reading in the 1930's, when Galsworthy was the grand old man, and Sinclair Lewis was at his peak, and Aldous Huxley and John Steinbeck were young, and John Erskine was having his greatest fun. Since then I've tapered off, by sheer necessity of time; but I sometimes wonder how much I'm missing, and fail to realize I'm missing, because I'm not in touch now as I used to be.

I had known Steinbeck as a gay friend and a struggling writer, who had achieved some notice with *Cup of Gold,* a slight novel about the buccaneer Sir Henry Morgan. I knew too that Steinbeck had written of his Mexican neighbors in *Tortilla Flat,* though he had had a fearful time finding a publisher. On New Year's Eve of 1934–1935 I asked him, "John, what are you working on now?" "I'm doing a book," he said, "about the leader of a cotton strike down in the San Joaquin Valley." That was, so far as I knew, a completely new departure for Steinbeck. "For heaven's sake," I pressed, "how did you get involved in anything like that?" "Why," he told me, "that's the livest thing that's happening just now." (The book was *In Dubious Battle,* less widely known than some of Steinbeck's others, but regarded by many critics as one of his very ablest.)

The livest thing that's happening, and the livest thinking about it, often may be revealed more livingly in the free scope of fiction than within the strict limits of factual reporting. We may not like what the novelist has chosen to tell: there were loud protests in both Oklahoma and California about *The Grapes of Wrath,* and I've gathered that some Southerners are not altogether happy about the South of William Faulkner. We may not like the point of view either: I still don't count *Elmer Gantry* to be quite the typical Methodist minister, and some of us may have been troubled by the gay and casual amorality of *The Private Life of Helen of Troy.*

These reactions of distaste do not wipe out the fact that people are writing and thinking thus. This is a datum of our twentieth century life to which the minister in the twentieth century will blind himself only on pain of excommunication from the twentieth century world. Nor does our disapproval erase, singlehanded, the social settings which the novelist portrays. The more we dislike their appearances, the more we are required to find out whether they really exist; and, in so far as they do turn out to be actual, to use our new apprehension of what is, in our effort to create what rather we believe should be.

38

Poetry

My Californians average out at a quarter of an hour of poetry a week, but 60 per cent of them record no reading of poetry at all. Here surely is a vacuum that needs to be filled, unless our lives are to lose much in beauty, truth, and goodness. It is a long while since most of us looked into Chapman's Homer, or any other version of the epics of pre-Athenian Greece. Another look well may put us again with the young Keats, "like some watcher of the skies/When a new planet swims into his ken." Vergil too is worth another try, and will help us to understand how the Romans felt when those upstart Christians dared to challenge the divine Emperor's dominion.

Dante and Milton, those crashing bores of the lower division lit. classes! But we were in the lower division then. One way to test whether we have climbed out of it is to determine whether the Divine Comedy means anything to us now, and whether in the Lost Paradise we can find any of the way toward its regaining. John Donne and George Herbert, left out of the anthologies on which we grew up, have come back to a life of the spirit as real in the reign of the second Elizabeth as it was in that of the first. Dryden and Pope meanwhile have moved into relative obscurity; but one who believes that the proper study of mankind is man will be ill content to leave them there.

Then there is the nineteenth century, and more in Wordsworth and Tennyson, in Longfellow and Lowell, than our early twentieth century teachers were willing to admit; and more in Walt Whitman, too, than most of those same teachers yet had discovered. The next great revival of interest, I suspect, will belong to Robert Browning. How's this, from "Bishop Blougram's Apology," for us who are trying to make the case for Christianity today?

> "What think ye of Christ," friend? when all's done and said,
> You like this Christianity or not?
> It may be false, but will you wish it true?
> Has it your vote to be so if it can?

And I find that my father carefully marked in his copy, which he was reading near the Great Wall of China in 1903,

> You own your instincts? why, what else do I,
> Who want, am made for, and must have a God
> Ere I can be aught, do aught?—no mere name
> Want, but the true thing with what proves its truth,
> To wit, a relation from that thing to me,
> Touching from head to foot—which touch I feel,
> And with it take the rest, this life of ours!
> I live my life here; yours you dare not live.

In our own day there have been high poetic visions too, even though at first we may be ill at ease in the absence of rhyme and of finger-counting meters. Catch up with Aldous Huxley as in "Orion," in 1931, he recorded his transit from futility to faith:

> The choice is ours, the choice is always ours,
> To see or not to see the living powers
> That move behind the numbered points and times.

See our Lord in our own daily living with the late Laureate Robert Bridges, in his valedictory *Testament of Beauty:*

> Thus unto all who have found their high ideal in Christ,
> Christ is to them the essence discern'd or undiscern'd
> of all their human friendships.

Lift up your heart in the revelation that came to a St. Louis bank clerk, as T. S. Eliot chants,

Suffer us not to mock ourselves with falsehood
Teach us to care and not to care
Teach us to sit still
Even among these rocks,
Our peace in His will.

Lean on the fence with New Hampshire's Robert Frost:

Before I built a wall I'd ask to know
What I was walling in or walling out . . .
Something there is that doesn't love a wall,
That wants it down.

Celebrate Christmas then with W. H. Auden:

He is the Way.
Follow Him through the Land of Unlikeness;
You will see rare beasts, and have unique adventures.

He is the Truth.
Seek Him in the Kingdom of Anxiety;
You will come to a great city that has expected
    your return for years.

He is the Life.
Love Him in the World of the Flesh;
And at your marriage all its occasions shall dance for joy.

The serious reading of poetry is not to be confused with
thumbing through cheap anthologies of cheap jingles, to
find a rounding-off tag line for a prosy sermon. Poetry offers
high adventure for the spirit. It lifts that spirit not out of
our daily living, but to new summits within it. Today, publishers say, poetry is a drug on the market; and even the
great houses are issuing each only one or two books of
verse in a year. Therein, however, we are protected in our
choice among the new offerings; and we have anyway full
three thousand years of treasure trove already at our hand,
if we will but seize upon it.

41

Drama as Reading

I failed to ask my Californians whether they devoted any time to the reading of plays, but I suspect the answer would have been even more largely negative than that for poetry. In the question period at Duke a theological student challenged me, and rightly, for having said nothing about the drama in a lecture series framed on analogies to the theater. There is more space in a book than there was time on the platform, and so we are free now to try a little filling of the gap.

The Greeks come first in time, and remain no worse than tied for first all these centuries after. The stern decrees of necessity troubled Aeschylus, but secured from him what he saw as his necessary assent. With more of sympathy for the individuals concerned, Sophocles wrestled with the same problems. Euripides rejected the old framework, fighting passionately for the rights of human individuals to be themselves. In *The Trojan Women* he laid bare the stupid brutality of the Trojan war, and in *The Bacchae* he caught the fire of individual religious ecstasy. Aristophanes, a fighting conservative, used the weapons of farce to assail the Euripidean innovations and the Socratic philosophy, and incidentally to probe human frailties of every kind. Not only heroic Greece and metropolitan Athens, but the human tragicomedy of every place and time, stands newly revealed as we come to know the Athenians who, writing of Greece, wrote also of us all.

The Latin theater was derivative, and its scanty remains have interest chiefly for specialized scholarship. This is not true of the mysteries and moralities of medieval England. Here the churchman is in a field very much his own, and one he will do well to cultivate. As he reads, he may

42

find himself impelled some time to produce for a Christmas festival the Coventry Nativity, or the Second Shepherds' play of Wakefield; and then he scarcely will be able to refrain from trying *Everyman* as a prelude to Lent. Lay Christianity in the Middle Ages was wondrously naïve, but it was no less wondrously genuine; and contact with it may help to spark genuineness in these more sophisticated times.

Shakespeare would be almost too obvious for mention, save that he rests on our shelves instead of coming alive in our hands. "I never knew Shakespeare quoted the Bible so much!" exclaimed a high-school girl whom, perhaps unwisely, I had taken to see John E. Kellerd in *Hamlet*. He quoted it rather little, in fact: much less than Chaucer did: but he said much that still has capacity to challenge, to inspire, and to cause to smile. Along with Shakespeare, at least Marlowe and Ben Jonson of the Elizabethans should be in every civilized man's repertoire of memory.

The next century was to be the great one in France. Few of us know anything of Jean Racine except the "War March of the Priests" which Mendelssohn wrote as incidental music for the Old Testament drama of *Athalie*. Racine was a Jansenist, and did also a dramatization of the life of Esther. Far more secular, but unquestionably more shrewd in his analysis of human foibles, was the actor-author Molière. Anyone whose parish is afflicted with pseudo-intellectuals or with hypochondriacs, to say nothing of the universally provenient genus of hypocrites, will be no end heartened by the dissection of these types in *Les Précieuses ridicules, Le Malade imaginaire,* and *Tartuffe.*

Goethe, like Racine, has suffered much from a musical misrepresentation. *Faust* in the Barbier-Carré libretto and with Gounod's Gallic setting is something altogether different from the play that Goethe wrote, and infinitely feebler. In particular we ought to know the tremendous second part, too often omitted from popular illustrated editions. Goethe finished this just before his death in 1832. Surely many a German, just a hundred years later, found himself echoing the words of the hero redeemed after so many failures and afflictions:

> Yes! to this thought I hold with firm persistence;
> The last result of wisdom stamps it true:
> He only earns his freedom and existence,
> Who daily conquers them anew.

Our age is inconceivable without the brilliant whimsy of George Bernard Shaw; and there is more than whimsy in his treatment of the martyr complex in *Androcles and the Lion,* and in his analysis of incipient nationalism in *Saint Joan.* The American needs to know Eugene O'Neill's New England redoing of the Oedipus myth in *Mourning Becomes Electra,* and his agonizing study of the fleeing Negro in *The Emperor Jones.* Thornton Wilder's *Our Town* is a tender and discerning portrait of anyone's upstate parish, filled with people whom we see every day, but may not have seen always with like compassion. T. S. Eliot, in his plays as in his poetry, at once uplifts and embarrasses. To which of the tempters in *Murder in the Cathedral* have we been the most prone to listen? How often, failing to think things through with the archbishop, have we been guilty of doing "the right thing for the wrong reason"?

Two fairly recent American plays will serve as samples for many others worth knowing. One is Arthur Miller's *Death of a Salesman,* which at first I was inclined to dismiss as a dully literal transcript from the empty life of the lower middle class, which almost all of us know at first hand. I learned, however, that not everyone had realized the horror of futility which that life involves for so many, and so I had to admit that Miller had opened the eyes of a large segment of the public to its own spiritual barrenness. The other, much gayer in its tone, seems also to have come as revelation to audiences and readers. *The Teahouse of the August Moon,* John Patrick's play from a novel by Vern Sneider, is one of the important sociological documents of our time. So long as we Americans can laugh at our own defeat in the cultural clash on Okinawa, so long there is hope that we shall see the world steadily and see it whole.

This addendum about the drama may be longer than it should have been, but any revising of it would be likely to issue only in further expansion. These plays I have mentioned I recommend without reservation. He who adventures further will find for himself many more that will prove equally rewarding; and he will know that the playwright has said many things which the preacher will do well to hear.

Reading for Fun

Are we permitted lighter reading in our lighter moments? By all means yes; and we are incomplete persons without it. Not poetry indeed, but important because refreshing light verse, came in an earlier day from Lewis Carroll and Sir W. S. Gilbert and Edmund Lear; and comes now from Ogden Nash and Dorothy Taylor and Phyllis McGinley. I could not do without Finley Peter Dunne's *Mr. Dooley* and Don Marquis's *archy and mehitabel,* and all of Robert Benchley and James Thurber, and I'm beginning to feel the same way about S. J. Perelman and Ludwig Bemelmans. Laughing with the world helps us alike toward understanding it, toward enduring it, and in loving it; and so the professional laugh maker has a rightful place along with the irrepressible amateur who lives next door.

As a college professor I was amazed, and more than a shade disappointed, to learn how little my clerical friends read murder mysteries. Only 3 per cent of the Californians admit to spending any time on "whodunits." I'm honestly sorry for the 97 per cent. No, the appeal is not the shedding of blood; and the highly improbable blondes of Mickey Spillane are only impeding nuisances to the true murder addict. What this very special genre gives, when it is properly done, is a perfect mathematical puzzle set in a perfectly impossible world; and so it is the best of specifics for putting a keyed-up and weary mind quietly to sleep.

Do we know that Dorothy Sayers, the creator of Lord Peter Wimsey, is also a distinguished theologian and a translator of Dante? Have we met the Roman convert G. K. Chesterton as creator and narrator of the blinking but perceptive Father Brown? Have we run across the social historian G. D. H. Cole, when, with the aid of his wife Margaret, he relaxes into straight detective doings? Have we heard that Nicholas Blake is the alter ego of the poet C. Day Lewis? These people are neither sensationalists nor fools; and I rise now in solemn defense of the academic profession, to declare that we who read their gorier works are not fools nor morbid maunderers either.

One of my colleagues, an associate professor of chemistry, finds his own light literature in the new field of science fiction. He is highly critical of me for not having tried it; and sooner or later I'll probably let myself be persuaded. I concede in advance that no doubt I shall find these books to be fun too—some day when I've really mastered all of Conan Doyle and Carter Dickson. Fun in reading? Why not? And if there must be some sort of rationalization, we may notice that our people do read the whodunits and the space stories, and that we ought by all means to be aware of what they're getting in them, for good or ill. As for me, that last is needless padding. The authentic mystery reader needs no excuse, and presents none.

Library and Ownership

How many books can a minister afford to own, as to either initial cost or shelf room? Here are two automatic stops for most of us. It becomes critically necessary, then, that we should choose wisely that which we shall decide to own and keep. The basic rule manifestly is that we must have, in permanent possession, everything to which we shall want to return with any frequency; and we can afford to leave to the library, public or university, the sort of thing that we shall read once only.

The minister needs first the Bible, and the more Bibles the better. He should have the Hebrew and Greek texts, at least for examination of particular passages and words, even if his reading of the scriptural originals is not as facile as he might wish. He must have the "King James," the American Standard, and the Revised Standard, for comparison among renderings at many a crucial point. To these he well may add the American Jewish translation, and the new Roman Catholic one which is being issued in sections by the Confraternity of Christian Doctrine.

He will profit greatly by owning also Moffatt's Bible and the Chicago "American" translation; and I would add at least the Twentieth Century, Weymouth, and Ballantine ("Riverside") New Testaments, and J. B. Phillips's renderings of the Gospels, the Epistles, and the Acts. The Bible was not antiquated when it was written, nor was it over-

47

cautious in its styling. The private versions, being of our own time and not subject to majority votes of committees, contribute vitality and freshness which sometimes are lacking from the "King James" because of its age, and from the Revised Standard because of its official character.

As introduction and commentary *The Interpreter's Bible* will be very nearly adequate in itself when all twelve of its volumes are available. A good analytical concordance and a reputable Bible dictionary are the other essential tools. Most of us will want more than this, but we don't need to buy every book about the Bible that appears. Careful examination in the bookshop or the library will do much to save us from false choices and needless cost.

Probably one ought to have a general Church History, and one of his own denomination, for quick reference. The growing life of the historic Church is helpfully illustrated, and at some points is richly presented, in "The Library of Christian Classics." For very rapid checking of details it is well to have on hand Vergilius Ferm's fairly new one-volume *Encyclopedia of Religion*. A standard, recent textbook of systematic theology will be a useful guide in the reading of the older sources; but never should its concise and over-simplified summaries be substituted for patient journeying through the classic treatments in their original forms.

Of devotional books, which will be discussed at some length in the final lecture, there are at least a dozen that every one of us ought to have always in reach. Worship materials, too, can be profitably multiplied. I would suggest that usually those issued by the standard churches are sounder and less sentimental than are the products of purely private initiative. (This is a different matter from that of the private renderings of the Bible, for in those the individual has no free range in the choice of content.) Two or three works on the methodology of worship should be available, and should be looked into every now and then, lest one grow stale in the crystallizing of his habits in the planning and leading of divine service.

As professional religionists, we shall need fewer permanent items in the collateral section. I would urge ownership of the basic works I have mentioned as "studies of man and society," from Plato to Spengler: we are going to need them more often than we can get conveniently to the library. There should be also one standard ancient history, one of Europe, one of the Oriental world, and one of the United States: and all of these certainly not older in original publication than the 1920's, for the writing of history has been greatly changed toward accuracy and objectivity in this half-century. A basic work in modern economics, one in sociology, and one each in biology and psychology and physics, ought always to be on hand for the checking of our vague impressions in these fields. Let me say that here I do not mean works about "religion and economics" or "religion and science." Some of these may be worth a reading or two; but it is only the solid and scholarly work in its own field of specialization, for the moment quite apart from religious connotations, that will give us a secure grounding in each particular area of knowledge.

Many of us will want to own copies of the poets and playwrights whom most we love, so that we can turn quickly to them in time of need. My own primary list is evident in the names and titles mentioned just above. Each of us will make his own; but each of us ought to do some new prospecting from time to time, lest he may be missing something that his spirit needs to grow on.

For the rest, there are the libraries. Even a small-town library has in it much worth investigating, and any eager reader can do a great deal to turn the book-buying policy in the direction of his own concerns. There are also county and state services to local units, greatly expanding the range of possible reading. University and seminary libraries, too, often look with a benevolent eye on off-campus clients, especially on those who manage a reasonably consistent promptness in returning what they have borrowed. My own inclination is to discount round-robin arrangements among friends, because I prefer on the whole to make my own selections; but I know some groups of clergy who have found this device not only financially convenient but also ideologically satisfying, especially when their reading has eventuated in group discussions.

The world is so full of a number of things that we ought jolly well to get better acquainted with it, and with them. The scene in which we are called to act is a busy and crowded one, confused and often confusing. The way out of confusion is understanding, and understanding rests upon knowledge.

Let us seek fully to know our scene in all its parts, and ever to learn more of the various characters who move about within it. Let us discover in detail how the scene was put together, in the long history of mankind. Let us identify its major supporting structures, in philosophy and in social institutions. Let us hear its authentic everyday speech in its novels, and its laughter in its comedians, and its noblest aspirations in its drama and its poetry.

We are in the world, and inescapably of it if creatively we would serve it. We need to know ourselves. We need no less to know our fellow man. This is why collateral reading is required in our clerical course of continuing study.

*   *   *

O GOD, the protector of all that trust in thee, without whom nothing is strong, nothing is holy: increase and multiply upon us thy mercy; that, thou being our ruler and guide, we may so pass through things temporal, that we finally lose not the things eternal. Grant this, O heavenly Father, for the sake of Jesus Christ our Lord. Amen.

—Gregorian Sacramentary, A.D. 590.

III

ADAPTING THE SCRIPT

Preparation for Services

> *GIVE grace, O heavenly Father, to all the ministers of thy Gospel, that they may, both by their life and doctrine, set forth thy true and lively Word, and rightly and duly administer thy holy Sacraments; through Jesus Christ our Lord. Amen.*
> —Adapted from the Prayer for the Church,
> Book of Common Prayer, A.D. 1549.

*   *   *

Up to this point we have been thinking of the ministerial rôle as receptive and largely passive, in the intake of our professional and collateral reading. But it is an active part that we have to play, and activity is of its essence even behind the scenes. The basic script and stage design are predetermined by our choice to serve the Christ in the world of men. The particular adaptations and adjustments remain to be made by each individual, and for his every appearance. We turn now to investigate the making of our direct, private preparation for the most public of our public duties.

My friends in California represent themselves as spending from two to twenty hours weekly in the preparing of their sermons, and from nothing to six hours in advance work on the services of worship. The average time reported for labor on sermons is nine hours and a half, and for the service one hour and three-quarters. What does not appear clearly (a fault in the planning of the questionnaire) is whether any of this time overlaps that which is devoted to reading. If the periods are mutually exclusive, the total desk time weekly for the average man adds up to some thirty hours: say six hours daily for a five-day week. That is heavy, in view of the numerous other things a parson has to do; but it is not impossible, and the demands of quality make it scarcely more than a minimum measure of what is desirable.

Unity of the Service

That the experience of worship in the church should be a unified and integrated one surely ought to go without saying. A haphazard collection of "preliminaries," followed by a sermon dissociated from them in atmosphere and content, may not be considered true "divine service." The planning by the minister must begin, therefore, with a careful consideration of the basic theme for each service, and preferably for related services in sequence over fairly extended periods. To this latter end it is necessary, every so often, to look ahead through the calendars, religious and secular, to see what special observances are coming and to determine how they should be fitted into the pattern as a whole.

There is sound reason for a large degree of structural identity from service to service, so that the worshipers will have the assurance of familiarity. For the same reason, the regular repeating of some congregational elements would seem to be normal: at least the Lord's Prayer and *Gloria Patri,* and I would say also the General Confession, the General Thanksgiving, and the basic chants and responses. There remain, however, within the standard structure even of an officially established ritual, a surprising number of options to be considered and decided for each day. Among these, along with the sermon, are hymns, responsive reading, lessons, anthems, and prayers.

No choice of any one of these is acceptable unless it is absolutely the best choice that can be made for the sake of the service as a whole. This requires on the minister's part both a general familiarity with Bible, hymnal, and service books (a familiarity which will increase steadily as his experience continues and widens), and for each particular occasion a special and patient searching of all the possible resources. Often it will be found that a hymn or a lesson set aside this time will be just right next week or the week after; and persisting work of this sort soon will free us from bondage to the hackneyed hymns and the cliché passages of Scripture.

Scarcely anyone but the preacher himself is qualified to make the detailed selection of materials which will ensure true unity in the hour of worship. (The guest preacher should be given this opportunity too, even though he is less well acquainted with the prior experiences and special habits of the congregation.) Ninety-two per cent of the Californians do their own choosing of the hymns, though one man secured his church's permission to do this only after two years of suffering through the banal and repetitious choices of the dominant layman in the local choir. An intelligent, informed, and consecrated choirmaster may be given the responsibility for hymn and anthem choices, on the basis of a careful briefing as to what each particular service is designed to become and to achieve; but at the best he must be subject to ministerial veto in cases where his judgment may contravene the subtle harmonies of mood that ought to be maintained. Organists commonly need encour-

54

agement, too, to live up to their own musical standards for prelude and postlude, against the sentimental and low-level demands of some members of the congregation.

If the preaching follows fairly closely the pattern of the Christian year, the standard lectionaries will provide useful aid toward the choice of Psalms and lessons. The revised American Episcopal lectionary of 1943 designates Psalms and both Old and New Testament lessons for Morning and Evening Prayer on every day of the year, with dual or triple alternates for Sundays and holy days. The lectionary in the Presbyterian *Book of Common Worship* (1946) supplies a two-year morning and evening cycle for Sundays and the major festivals, with a Psalm and Old and New Testament lessons for each. In *A Book of Worship for Free Churches* (Congregational, 1948) there will be found a similar scheme, though without provision for any evening service. *The Book of Worship* (Methodist, 1945) gives two lessons for each Sunday and for a few holy days, but almost always Epistle and Gospel instead of Old and New Testament. (Actually there are only seven Old Testament lessons specified, four of them from Isaiah and one each from Zechariah, Joel, and Jeremiah.) Dr. G. Phillips Osborn in *Christian Worship: A Service Book* (Disciples, 1953) offers a five-year scheme of New Testament lessons and Psalms, again apparently for a single service each week.

The lectionary need not be a dictator, but it can be a very helpful guide. Surely, however, the question of the use of the Old Testament needs to be reëxamined. It is a curious phenomenon that in Protestantism, which professes to find its highest authority in holy Scripture, the actual reading of the Scriptures so often is cut to a minimum, and thus that the noble Hebrew heritage of Christianity is frequently ignored in our services. Three-dimensional vision requires the focusing of two lenses on the object; and a rounded view of any religious problem or value is the more likely to be secured if we see it through the earlier Jewish lens as well as the later Christian one.

For every legitimate subject of Christian preaching there is, within the vast wealth of the Biblical materials, something relevant and illumining in both the Old Testament and the New. Coupled with the use of the lectionaries there needs to be that practice of the serious, consecutive, actively curious reading of the Bible which was discussed in our opening inquiry. A concordance may help too, and also the marginal references in a study edition. To find the most appropriate lessons possible, and to be sure that they are the most appropriate, will require much of time and labor. To be content with anything less fitting is to waste the time of the people when they are gathered to worship God and to hear his truth.

Just 25 per cent of the Californians say that they write out the prayers which they use in the services, and 3 per cent more indicate that they depend upon prayers from standard service books. If this means that 72 per cent give no thought to their praying with the congregation until the prayer is to be offered, it betrays an unhappy situation. The unprepared prayer, however eloquent it may sound, scarcely can avoid being limited in scope, repetitive in theme, and banal in phrasing. The general concerns of the congregation ought always to be brought before the Lord; but this can be done largely, and most helpfully, by broadening the range of unison prayers of the people themselves. The special intent of the day likewise is a proper and necessary object of our praying. Thoughtful planning of its expression will aid greatly toward bringing people to the throne of the heavenly grace with this particular concern consciously in their minds and actively in their hearts.

Whether the spoken prayers be dominantly ancient ones, or the composition of the minister for the specific occasion, they will fail to become the prayers of the congregation unless their content, order, and placing in the service are carefully worked out in the quiet of the study. In general a series of short, specific petitions has more clarity and vital force than has a long and apparently undivided discourse to the Almighty. The traditional "collect" form is worth studying, with its address, petition, and conclusion; and, as I have suggested elsewhere, the effort to imitate it often will issue profitably in our giving up the effort, and employing instead the apter phrasing of the prayers that reflect the deepest feelings of the Church down the long reach of the Christian centuries.

One valuable consequence of preparing prayers before the service is that they are the more likely to be real prayers directed to the Almighty, and less homilies aimed at the congregation. The distinction here is a subtle one, for manifestly the spoken prayer is intended to direct the hearers' attention and to secure their assent. This, however, is to the chief end that they themselves shall be praying. To ensure this result we must exercise the greatest care in selecting the words in which each of our prayers shall be expressed.

Even the benediction may be chosen consciously, and used significantly, to bring together the meaning of the whole hour of worship. There is no need that we shall limit ourselves to the two or three most familiar forms of "dismissal." The Scriptures are full of other passages which as they stand, or with very slight adaptations, will bring the service to its close on a note of specific consecration and challenge, in terms of the particular aspect of our faith to which the thought of that service has been devoted. In the ancient liturgies, also, there will be found a number of moving and uplifting forms of final blessing. Once more a considerable amount of searching, thinking, and choosing is indicated. Once more the results will fully justify the effort.

For most Protestants the one hour on Sunday morning is their total experience of public worship within the week. How solemn, then, is the obligation that rests upon us as leaders of worship to make every moment of that hour fully significant for every individual present. Our hope of even approximate attainment of the goal rests upon our willingness to spend many hours in making the one hour's script altogether appropriate and completely ready.

Planning the People's Part

The service of worship is not a performance by minister and choir, with the congregation present merely as audience. If the people actually are to take part in the worship, however, the means to their doing so must be placed conveniently within their reach. Here to date the Anglicans and the Lutherans have a great advantage over the rest of us, for the full texts of their services always are available to every worshiper: for the Anglicans in *The Book of Common Prayer,* for the Lutherans bound together with their hymnal. Most of us have seen the validity of this principle, hitherto, only in the case of the hymns and the Psalter. But if the people are to pray together with one voice, they need prayer books in their hands just as surely as they need hymnals for their singing together.

Very few local Presbyterian, Methodist, and Congregational churches have placed copies of their official worship books in the pews. Only this spring a Congregational minister expressed great surprise when I suggested that this should be done. "It never occurred to me," he said, "that our *Book of Worship* was meant to be used by anyone but the minister." Yet that book is full of congregational prayers and responses which are null and void as congregational material unless the congregation has access to them. In the same way the magnificent new (and mostly ancient) Communion liturgy in the Presbyterian *Book of Common Worship* is pathetically incomplete when its congregational parts are said by the celebrant only or, as sometimes happens, are left out altogether.

Perhaps a certain amount of backstage talking on the parson's part, in selling key individuals in the parish on the revolutionary idea of buying prayer books in equal quantity with hymnals, would be appropriate here. Publicly too, before his board or session, and before the whole congregation, he will need to make the case for this means to the fullness of the people's sharing. Until there dawns the happy day when he wins the argument, and the supply is unpacked and placed in the racks, the weekly leaflet provides something of a surrogate.

Probably the leaflet is desirable anyway, to specify the variable parts of the service and thereby to preclude the interruptions of recurring announcements. It can be smaller, simpler, and less expensive if it is a supplement to the prayer book rather than a substitute for it. In either case it should be literate and, within the necessary limits of space, informative. The author and composer of a hymn and its tune, and their dates, ought always to be noted; and gradually the people will come to expect this information and to think about it. (No, they can't be expected to look themselves for the data printed at the top of the hymns: let us not hope for the impossible.) Similarly it is well to provide a quiet reminder of the sources and dates at least of the major congregational prayers, and a line suggesting something of the background and nature of the day's lessons.

Some of the space commonly devoted to parish affairs and promotional interests, and especially that used for the now fashionable front-page essay by the pastor, well might be diverted to the nobler end of enriching the general understanding of our services and of their constituent parts. An illuminating mimeographed leaflet is better than an unenlightening printed one; and the normal low cost of mimeographing, in view of the almost universal possession of mimeographs by our churches, will permit a great expansion of usefulness with no great increase, and quite possibly a reduction, in total expense.

Here again hard work is essential, and hard work done well ahead of time. The choices have to be made, the data checked, the copy prepared, early enough to permit careful and accurate reproduction. A week before the given service is none too early for full readiness; and this means that the enterprise should be begun a full week before that. It can be done if we believe it is worth doing. If we don't do it, we have little right to expect that our services will become the authentic, active worshiping of all of our people.

Preparing for Shorter Services

Traditionally, American Protestantism has held few services without sermons, but in all our churches we are holding more than we used to. The most important is the celebration of the Holy Communion, seen as a sacrament needing no sermon for its validation. Baptism frequently occurs at a separate service, and marriage almost always. Confirmation (or its equivalent) is gaining ground as an important ceremony, and new rituals are being devised for a great variety of occasions in the church's life and in the Christian's.

Since the forms of most of these observances are relatively fixed, there is a strong temptation to suppose that they can be carried out from the book without much, or any, prior consideration. Here in particular the Anglicans seem often to be entrapped by that prayer book which in so many ways is their special treasure. One hears the wrong collect begun and halted, and a new start made; the epistle garbled because its text has not been examined beforehand; and a painful silence occurring while the cleric searches two pages for a fitting offertory sentence, or fumbles overleaf to see whether the day has a proper preface. Similarly, and in all denominations, there are hitches at weddings because the minister's memory has failed him on personal names, or on whether there will be one ring or two.

No matter how regular the general pattern and phrasing, each service we hold is unique, and should be treated as a new adventure in our approach to God. A half-hour Communion needs almost certainly more than half an hour before it to make sure of its exact content, and of the celebrant's fullest possible understanding of each element in the day's structure. Baptism is an ancient rite of the Church, but it is a once-in-a-lifetime experience for the individual to be baptized. The individual therefore must be considered in the following of the rite, with that gospel passage

61

chosen which best fits his age and spiritual development, and with easy assurance rather than hesitation in beginning either the infant or adult series of questions.

Too many people in our modern society get to church only for weddings and funerals. Perhaps more of them would come more often if they found those services at once graceful in their production and full of grace in their meaning. It is inexcusable for a minister to botch a marriage ceremony, and it is insult to man and blasphemy toward God if he is confused or incoherent at a burial.

At least for marriages and burials, and on occasion for baptisms too, the safest procedure is to copy out the full service in a consecutive whole, with all minor variations and personal references included just as they are to be used. By this technique we are guarded against misplaced pronouns ("him" for "her" with reference to a girl baby) and muddled proper names ("Marion" when the bride is "Marilyn"), and at the same time we avoid all shuffling of pages. If the copy itself is made physically attractive, it will be a welcome gift to the family after the service is over; and they will appreciate it the more because already the service has approved itself to them by its decency and order, and by its consequent religious significance.

I personally type out in full every service that I conduct, except Communions without music or sermon; and for those I read over the full text carefully and put markers at all the necessary places in the book. Often beforehand the copying seems to be a terrible chore: how many times in the years have I typed the General Confession? During the service, however, the new and exact copy is a source of strength and assurance, permitting me to give full attention to meanings without any worry about the finding of places. Again there is a secondary advantage, if carbons can be made and handed to organist, choirmaster, and any lay reader(s) who may be involved. Their resultant gain in confidence is greater even than the minister's, and may make even more difference in the smoothness of the whole.

Choosing Sermon Subjects

"How long did it take you to write that book?" The only possible answer for any author is, "All my life to the date I sent the script in." It takes just as long for the writing of a sermon. The reason is that what a man will preach about, and how he will preach about it, are determined by the totality of his experience in the Christian life and in everything he ever has seen and known. Within this experiential matrix he must look for the choices he has to make for each several year and for each particular Sunday.

There is a matrix larger still, in the one ongoing cause which all of us are committed to serve. The theme of all Christian preaching is the gospel of Christ, which is the power of God unto salvation. That theme is so great, and its reach so inclusive, that we never shall come near to saying about it all that is true of it. Within the one theme there are infinite ramifications of detail, far more numerous than one lifetime of preaching may begin to encompass.

The first and most useful guide to the choosing of particular subjects is the Christian calendar. This provides a systematic arrangement of the field of Christian thought, turning our attention to one aspect after another of the plan of salvation. The historic sequence of the church year, long ignored by nonconformists, is regaining attention because it has become evidently needed. Following it through in order, we shall be preserved alike from omitting any vital consideration, and from concentrating more than is necessary on a few points that specially have caught our individual attention.

Christmas and Easter long have had almost universal recognition in our churches, even those which once rejected the calendar as "popish." Whitsunday, the Day of Pentecost, is being widely rediscovered. Along with these days of special joy in salvation and grace, there is the necessary balance provided by the Lenten season of the sinner's self-scrutiny and penitence, with its culmination in the solemn vigil at the cross on Good Friday. These at least ought to be the themes of services and sermons in every church every year, and they will establish the framework upon which all our other preaching will depend.

American custom has added Thanksgiving Day, Independence Day, and Mother's Day, as quasi-ecclesiastical feasts practically everywhere observed. It is well for the Church to claim these, if it uses them to insist upon a validly Christian approach to each. Is our thanksgiving one of smug contentment or of humble reconsecration? Is our patriotism combative or creative? Are our mothers worshiped as the minor saints which most of them aren't, or recognized as the earnest but troubled humans that they are? In the same way the common recognition of Lincoln's and Washington's birthdays may have value and promote Christian purposes, or may contribute to nothing but the anti-Christianity of party and national pride, depending on whether their interpretation is Christian or patrioteering.

At the same time we should remember that the Church has days of its own whose reference is more authentically Christian than that of these American holidays, and heroes whose service was not to a single fatherland but to the universal brotherhood in Christ Jesus. Trinity Sunday in late spring, the Ascension Day in the summer, All Saints' and All Souls' Days in mid-autumn, seldom are noted in most of our churches. Surely they merit more attention among Christians than do merely national feasts and/or new and commercially promoted celebrations. In every year some major saints' days will fall on Sundays, and will provide special opportunity at once to instruct and to inspire those who owe to the saints of God more than they know.

In addition to the subjects suggested by these special occasions, the lectionaries will be found recurringly fruitful in sermon ideas; and as they are planned in continuing and organic relationships, they will aid in keeping the scheme of preaching orderly and coherent. This paragraph is being written in the week before the Fifth Sunday after Trinity (Anglican, Lutheran, Presbyterian, Congregational), which is the Sixth Sunday after Pentecost (Roman Catholic, Methodist). As we see what this one day has to offer, let us remember that every other Sunday of the year is similarly rich in varied and vital suggestion.

The Presbyterian morning materials in the "second year" series include the stirring seventh chapter of Amos ("I was no prophet . . . the Lord took me"); I Corinthians 6 ("ye are washed . . . ye are sanctified . . . ye are justified"); a part of the Lukan version of the Sermon on the Mount; and the Johannine discourse on the unity of the Son with the Father. The Congregational references ("first year") are to Jeremiah's promise of restoration; to the same Pauline passage as in the Presbyterian listing; and to the end of St. Matthew's text of the great Sermon. The Methodist choices are this last and (one of the few Old Testament passages included) Zechariah's "the streets of the city shall be full of boys and girls playing." For Morning Prayer the Episcopal selections include passages from Genesis, Proverbs, Ecclesiastes, St. Matthew, Hebrews, and St. James. The Epistle for both Anglicans and Lutherans is from I St. Peter, "if ye suffer for righteousness' sake, happy are ye"; and the Gospel is St. Luke's account of the miraculous draught of fishes.

Where now is the man who had trouble finding something to preach about this next Sunday? If he likes none of these, he has available for scrutiny three more Presbyterian sets, one Congregational, and three Anglican, provided for this one day of the year. This year he has St. Peter's Day in the same week, with its challenge for a Protestant interpretation of "upon this rock I will build my church."

He has also whatever stimulus any of these may give him to mark out new sequences of his own. Isn't Amos a natural starter for a series on the prophets, and St. Peter for one on the apostles? The theology of St. Paul can be profitably examined for a number of weeks, and in deep devotion as well as in accurate scholarship. The Sermon on the Mount is standard material for series treatment, but it never yet has been wrung dry. Jeremiah and St. John are treasuries whose riches are inexhaustible. Put now with the lectionaries that persistent individual reading of the Scriptures already mentioned, and the embarrassment of our wealth is even more apparent. There are not enough weeks in a year, nor in a lifetime, for us to discuss even a small portion of the Biblical revelation that offers itself to be studied with our people.

"Topical" in our common parlance has come to be understood as meaning "non-Biblical." Here some careful distinguishing is required, between religious subjects that are rooted in the Bible as a whole even if not clearly in a single passage, and secular topics with or without a Biblical text inserted to imitate sermon form. Theology obviously needs often to be discussed, and much of the theology of the Church is a relatively late flowering from the Biblical roots. Christian ethics in the modern world belong to religion, and so belong to the pulpit. Here again the Scriptures, written in other and quite different cultural settings, do not give us all the detail we need for today's implementing of their principles. Sermons on events in church history, or on individual heroes of post-Biblical times, similarly involve a relatively smaller proportion of Biblical reference and a larger one of supplementary data.

The illegitimate "topical" sermon is the secular essay which some have thought justified in the attempt to win crowds. The trouble is that it does not influence people toward anything of any import. A good deal of pulpit book reviewing falls under this condemnation, and some preaching of the social gospel is less gospel than it is tendentious sociology and politics. Perhaps the besetting sin of the pulpit in this decade has been the substitution of psychology for religion, especially in the emphasis on seeking God for individual advantage rather than on serving him because he is Lord of all. Certainly we need to relate our Christian faith and morals to the current scene, social and intellectual. What always we must be sure of is that it is Christianity, and not mere contemporaneity, that provides the motive for our choosing of subjects and that determines the detail of our sermon preparation.

The thoughtful preacher will consider, among all the other factors, the existing interests of his own congregation. In some areas of religious concern they won't know enough to ask significant questions, and here of course the initiative will have to come from the pulpit. There is more of active theological curiosity among laymen, however, than many of the clergy yet have realized—if one may judge their estimate by their weekly sermon announcements in the newspapers. A simple and useful testing may be made by circulating return post cards for sermon suggestions. My own experience with this is that few trivial questions are asked, and a high proportion of eager and penetrating ones. This last year the questions received by mid-November allowed the making out of a full sermon schedule up to June; and its fulfillment brought up a host of new sermon ideas to be filed away for a "some day" that may or may not come.

The Process of Preparation

The specific preparing of a sermon begins as soon as its topic is decided. To know what one proposes to speak about sets him thinking in that direction, and enables him to catch in flight any passing idea, reference, or illustration that may turn out to be relevant. Starting "cold" on final or near-final production is likely to mean slow work and a thin product. Thinking on any theme goes better when the motors have been warmed up by advance awareness, even if not always at the highest level of consciousness. This means that we shall do our better sermonizing when we make our schedules reasonably far ahead, and so make ourselves receptive in each of the areas we have selected for discussion.

The basic material for a Biblically oriented sermon has provided itself in the choosing of the subject. The given passage needs to be read carefully and prayerfully many times, and in as many translations as possible. Its handling in at least one dependable commentary ought then to be checked, for the sake of completeness and accuracy in one's own treatment. Often the Bible Dictionary too will help, especially in the identifying of cognate materials in other parts of the Scriptures.

The minister's library is likely to contain relevant books, chapters, essays, or sermons, both ancient and modern. If he has access to a good public or academic library, and time enough for searching in it, he may find further enrichment for his mind before he fixes on his own particular approach. Such materials the preacher ought to read freely, but never to quote in any large measure, and of course not at all without giving due credit.

There is, one fears, too much of not quite unconscious plagiarism in the modern pulpit. Reading books of sermons is all very well for information and for the stirring up of ideas, but it is a menace when it becomes a substitute for one's own thinking. What Shakespeare's Touchstone says of his Audrey should be every honest preacher's boast: "A poor thing, but mine own." Our own sermons, actively thought out and prayerfully related to our own people's needs, never can be such poor things as are the local imitations of what some big-city preacher said (or what his book says he said) to his big-city congregation. We who write books love to have them used: used, but not reproduced. Copying is no compliment to us, for it shows that we have failed to stimulate creative imagination on the reader's part.

Personal habits cannot but vary as to the making and using of a filing system for projected future reference. Some men preserve and classify large numbers of clippings, and a few men can find the item they want when they want it. A larger and more flexible file is the purely mental

one, growing day by day as one reads and thinks, and providing its own tabs to pull out one or another thread of
recollection. The more one knows, say, of St. Augustine,
the more quickly he identifies a remembered sentence as
being typically Augustinian; and the more thoroughly he
has read John Wesley, the more readily he will know where
in Wesley's works to look for the exact phrasing of a pun-
gent piece of advice to a young preacher.

The California questionnaire shows 44 per cent who write
out their sermon scripts in full, and 56 per cent who do
not. The average times of preparation reported are twelve
hours weekly for the former and eight hours for the latter:
the four extra hours being probably a fair representation
of the time required for the physical job of writing. That is
half a normal working day. Is its usefulness enough to
justify one's spending it in this manner?

My own experience through thirty-five years from my
first sermon has led me to reply emphatically "Yes." In
common with most of the clergy, I have a reasonably facile
tongue. That is just the difficulty. It is too facile, when
uncontrolled by prior planning, for my speaking to be
exact, balanced, and decently brief. I respectfully suggest
that this may be true of others as well as myself.

When I did experiment with extempore preaching, some
twenty-five years ago, I realized in particular that I wasn't
handling transitions gracefully and clearly. There was
also the problem of repetitiousness, alike within a single
sermon and from week to week. It is hard enough in writing,
and it is almost impossible in casual speaking, adequately
to limit one's use of his own favorite, habitual, stereotyped
phrases. (This is what makes preacher and professor both
such easy marks for lampooning in youth fellowship and
student skits.) It is frustrating, too, to find one's self wonder-

ing when last one told the pet story, or just where one used the smashing poem. And the problem of brevity may be the most serious one of all, for public speech always is longer for any hearer than it is for the speaker.

From my late father I imitated the practice I still use, of writing each script first in longhand and then on the typewriter. The longhand is much more readily adjustable while the piece is in its first and fluid stages. Once that copy is complete, and has been duly marked with excisions, substitutions, transpositions, and insertions, it can be reproduced in the neater and more legible form which the machine provides.

During the typing I revise further, though usually now on a smaller scale. One trick here is to put in monosyllables for polysyllables if I can, and Saxon words for Latin and Greek ones. Another is to try to cut compound sentences in two. Then comes an interim of several days at least, allowing at its end a fresh and more critical look at the product. Normally one more typing completes the job, though I may do a total of three or four if I find myself more than ordinarily unhappy about the general movement and the specific wording.

No two men will work in exactly the same way; and individual variations in temperament, in verbal memory, in writing facility, and not least in typing skill, will require considerable variation in the detail of procedure. The fact remains that we can not be certain of what we are going to say in the pulpit unless we make certain beforehand. The Holy Ghost indeed may inspire us suddenly, anywhere and at any time; but the Holy Ghost works in us through our regular mental processes, and therefore most helpfully when we put our minds most carefully, completely, and purposefully at his service.

The Sermon in the Service

The wheel comes now full circle to the point where this study began: that of the organic unity of the whole service, and the character of the sermon as but one of the important elements contributing to its total impact. This means that both the subject and the tone of its treatment are to be tested by their service or disservice to the people's worship of God. Flippancy and cheapness are nowhere to be desired or admired, but they are least of all permissible in the time assigned to the setting forth of God's truth and God's will.

This does not mean that laughter as such is necessarily out of place. Humor is a powerful weapon against human stupidity and stuffiness, and it can be also a helpful builder of a sense of social oneness. Here, by the way, is yet another argument for writing, for it is the impromptu witticism that is most likely to hurt without intention. The comedy should be implicit in the situation, and it will continue to be funny when the sermon is delivered if it was genuinely funny when first it occurred to the writer. The irrelevant or labored joke, inserted merely to wake up the hearers, belongs to the professional comic and not to the preacher of Christ.

Looking out from the midweek's backstage to Sunday's public appearance, the preacher will decide whether to work in public with the script or without it. Reading is the safest way to ensure that none of the preparation made shall be wasted, and that no extraneous materials will slip in. It is possible, if one has the material fully at his command, to read without disturbing the congregation by evident bondage to the sheets of paper. Our people know today, from radio and TV, that national figures always use scripts when they make pronouncements of any importance. They may therefore be the more ready to attach importance to the script which God's ambassador has prepared in his service to God and man.

Word-by-word memorizing, conversely, is dangerous and can be self-defeating. The memorizer, trying to give the impression of eloquent extemporaneity, almost inevitably betrays by the tone of his voice that he is not thinking but merely reproducing. If his memory fails him when he is not really thinking, there will be one of those distressful breaks that afflict competitors in high-school speaking contests.

Outline notes sometimes may be helpful, if the sermon includes a number of correlative items that need to be kept in the right sequence. Notes are at least as conspicuous as a full script, however; and they become more so when the preacher has to pause to find his place in them. On the whole the better procedure, if one has an unconquerable aversion to taking the script into the pulpit, is to depend on no memoranda other than those held in a clear and ordered mind. If one really has thought the sermon through, if he actually has its prepared content under control, he will come very close to reproducing what he has written while with his people he is thinking it through again.

Whether or not one proposes to read, his preparation must provide assurance that he knows his material thoroughly: its structure, its specifications, its inner relationships. A careful job of writing and revising will go a long way toward guaranteeing this. How much private rereading may be necessary will vary with the individual, and individual experience will give the answer to each of us. Be we well assured, however, that less than the minimum we personally require will result in less than maximum usefulness of the sermon in the service.

We are imperfect persons, whose adapting of the scripts of Christian truth never will attain to perfection. Full awareness of this should drive us to our knees in contrition for our inadequacies, and in humble petition that we shall achieve the best that in us lies. If we have prayed sincerely we then shall work faithfully. Then, and only then, may we hope that new light will break forth out of God's word as we rehearse it and seek to interpret it.

The conclusion of the matter is Martin Luther's sacristy prayer, which we at Mills learned from the Chapel of Gettysburg Seminary, and a copy of which confronts each of our ministers in those last moments behind the scenes before the time comes for him to go out to meet and serve the people of God.

*　　*　　*

O LORD GOD, dear Father in heaven, I am, indeed, unworthy of the office and ministry in which I am to make known thy glory and to nurture and to serve this congregation.

But since thou hast appointed me to be a pastor and teacher, and the people are in need of the teachings and the instructions, O be thou my helper and let thy holy angels attend me.

Then if thou art pleased to accomplish anything through me, to thy glory and not to mine or to the praise of men, grant me, out of thy pure grace and mercy, a right understanding of thy Word and that I may, also, diligently perform it.

O Lord Jesus Christ, Son of the living God, thou Shepherd and Bishop of our souls, send thy Holy Spirit that he may work with me; yea, that he may work in me to will and to do through thy divine strength according to thy good pleasure. Amen.

—Martin Luther, A.D. 1483–1546.

IV

KEEPING IN CONDITION

Recreation

SINCE it is of thy mercy, O gracious Father, that
another day is added to our lives; we here dedicate
both our souls and our bodies to thee and thy service,
in a sober, righteous, and godly life; in which resolu-
tion do thou, O merciful God, confirm and strengthen
us; that, as we grow in age, we may grow in grace, and
in the knowledge of our Lord and Saviour Jesus
Christ. Amen.

—Edmund Gibson, A.D. 1705.

*　　*　　*

Trust me, To-day's Most Indispensables,
Five hundred men could take your place or mine.

Rudyard Kipling in "The Last Department" was writing
of the civil service in India, but his judgment applies equally
to any other field of activity—in the long run. There are
a few occupations, however, for which in the short run
individual replacements are not easy to secure and never
can be identical. Foremost among these are the stage and
the church.

A theatrical star has an understudy ready to take over
in an occasional emergency. Only rarely does the understudy achieve any popular triumph, and commonly the star's
long incapacity will put an end to the run of the play. The
minister in the typical parish has no understudy at all,
and seldom is there an adequate substitute who can be

75

secured overnight. Both actor and cleric therefore carry a special obligation, to themselves and their respective constituencies, never to miss a show or a service. This means that, beyond most men, these never can afford the luxury of being out of commission.

The affirmative side of their situation is that always they have to be fit, always must keep in condition. Physically and mentally alike they must be as nearly as possible at their best for every appearance they make. They mustn't be sick, mustn't be weary, mustn't be out of temper. Yet their jobs are demanding, their human contacts are fraying to the nerves, the strains under which they work are severe and well-nigh ceaseless. It follows that they must give particular attention to securing rest, relaxation, and refreshment, whenever their schedules will allow a moment's change of pace. This evidently is why the Duke committee suggested that one of the lectures should be devoted to an inquiry into the minister's recreational life.

Exercise

A recent bulletin of the Duke Divinity School, in a happy memorial tribute to that grand old man Professor Ernest Findlay Scott, quoted as his first rule for attaining a healthy longevity, "Under no circumstances take any exercise whatever." There are times when we all may be inclined to regard this as sound counsel. I have long contemplated writing an extended and enthusiastic essay on "The Virtues of Horizontality," elaborating the propositions, "Never stand when you can sit, and never sit when you can lie down." Our department of Health and Physical Education at Mills every now and then prescribes "Rest" as a semester's "activity" for a rundown or hyperthyroid girl; and there is a series of campus jokes about flunking "Elementary Rest" and so failing of promotion to the course in "Intermediate Rest."

Some of us need to ponder that. If we do not master Elementary Rest, we are disqualified from engaging aright even in Elementary Activity. There is nothing to be proud of in being perpetually or even regularly tired. To say that we are worn out with our labors is to announce that we've made a poor fist of planning our time and controlling our schedules, and quite possibly also that we don't really enjoy our work. A good night's sleep is a prerequisite for a good day's output; and if the night is inescapably cut by a late meeting at one end of it, and an early service at the other, an afternoon nap is clearly indicated for catching up.

The fit body nevertheless does need movement as well as repose, and thus something of what we call "exercise" ordinarily has a rightful place in our schedules. I'll venture the guess that the late Dr. Scott, being of Scottish origin, was capable of one form of exercise beyond most of his American friends, and took it so much as a matter of course that he didn't notice its exercising function. I refer to the lost art of walking.

Here I speak inevitably with the prejudice of an ex-Briton, and of one who in recent years has abjured the ownership of an automobile. Certainly a residence college campus offers special advantages here, in its brief distances and its pleasant pathways. I cheat a bit too, with the result that last fall a freshman asked a senior, "Who's that funny old man on the bicycle?" But I can and do walk as well, and not on the campus only.

I recommend specifically the downtown walk, which combines healthy physical activity with sociological discovery and thrilling human contact. My favorite procedure on a day off is to take a bus to some part of Oakland or San Francisco that I don't know well, and then just to start walking. While the lungs and muscles are getting a painless workout, the eye gains a new perspective on the community, the mind works subconsciously both in the immediate scene and on forthcoming times of active duty, the heart is at once touched by human need and warmed by human friendliness.

In the small town one doesn't have to drive to the post office or the luncheon club every time. A walk from parsonage to shopping area, at the cost of a very few extra minutes, may pay off richly in toning up the psychic as well as the physical mechanism. Nor will the oil companies go bankrupt from some cutting of the stop-start wastage of gasoline that goes with short-distance driving.

Another happy way of using and developing energy, without the need of elaborate prearrangement and with a completely optional terminus, is available just outside the front and back doors. There is a sound rule that no man should plant more garden than his wife can tend. It will help both his body and his soul, however, if he does some of the pruning and weed pulling on his own account. There is a deep satisfaction in seeing a plot newly cleared, even a plot of a very few square feet. There is happy excitement when the first shoots peep through the soil, or the first red-brown leaves on the roses promise the rich green foliage of later spring. There is legitimate pride in the gay blooming of the summer, for him who knows that he was God's partner in the enterprise of production.

A special virtue of the garden is that, while it makes varying demands upon physical prowess, it almost never claims all of one's mental energy. Without necessarily trying to think, the gardener finds himself thinking. Many a sermon has taken shape, many a plan has been developed, many a problem in human relations has been worked out, while the iris were being divided or the new geranium slips were being set out alongside the path. Any garden can use a full-time worker, and no minister's garden will get one. But the garden is so tolerant that it welcomes whatever attention it can secure, and it repays that attention richly alike in its own growing and in the gardener's.

The extent to which a man can engage in the more active sports and games depends upon a combination of circumstance and physique. A YMCA or a clubhouse may provide for volleyball, swimming, or badminton, and for an almost automatic availability of associates. Tennis demands an opponent, and golf is dull without one; which usually means advance gearing of disparate schedules. Some will find it possible to set a regular weekly time with one friend or more; but the exigencies of the clerical life are almost certain to cause a considerable number of suddenly broken dates. Team games are a fortiori even more difficult to get into, unless there is a local church league in basketball, softball, or something comparable.

A special responsibility is laid upon the minister when he assumes the rôle of a sports competitor. He of all men must hold the ego in check, must keep a firm grip on the original sin that tends so readily to break out in slightly unfair tactics or in seriously angry temper. I saw a young parson playing for his church in a basketball league. His team was behind in a crucial game, and he got a little too overenthusiastic. As he charged down the court and bowled over a much smaller opponent, a voice arose from the opposition's bench: "Hey, mister! Ya dropped yer Bible!" We are not permitted to drop our Bibles, whatever the temptation or the provocation; and this is something to keep actively in mind on the eighteenth green.

Amusements

Spectator sports draw large crowds, and clergy among them. Years ago I had a regular pass to Pacific Coast League baseball games, but I gave up asking for it because it tempted me more than I was able to bear. The local high-school games commonly are nearer than the professional ones, they cost less, and often they are more fun anyway. They carry the added advantage of providing an extra and happily shared experience within the home community. If one can get to a big league park once in a while, or perhaps to one major football game in a season, these are stirring in themselves and constitute excellent conversation pieces in the younger group. One man had to teach himself, however, in his student pastor days, a special technique of yelling for the Southern California Trojans on Saturday afternoons so as not completely to ruin his vocal chords for Sunday morning.

A young cleric who read a preliminary draft of this lecture caught a serious omission at this point. He says he became interested in big league baseball because he was interested in his young people and therefore in what interested them. In consequence he began to read the sports pages in the newspapers, and now he subscribes to *Sports Illustrated* simply because he enjoys it. I believe he's right on both counts; and I pass along his counsel that we ought to read the sports news regularly, alike for the sake of our contact with our young people and with our men of every age, and for the sake of our own adrenal glands.

Times have changed since some of us were young, and

the mood of our churches about the permissibility of a Christian's attending commercial amusements is completely different from what it was a generation ago. We were of course superbly inconsistent then. The theater had been for almost four centuries under the Puritan ban; but the motion picture, having been invented after the reasons for disapproval of the legitimate stage long had been forgotten, was not placed under anything like the same condemnation.

While I was serving my first charge, I went to a play of the old Morosco stock company in Los Angeles, and in the foyer ran into a family from the church. "Why, Mr. Hedley, what are you doing here?" They seemed puzzled by my replying, "The same thing you are: seeing the play." There is a sort of poetic justice in the sequel: namely, that thirty years later the granddaughter of that same family was a major in Speech and Drama at Mills College, and that I had the pleasure of acting with her in a campus production of Molière's *The Miser*.

"All things are lawful unto me, but all things are not expedient." St. Paul repeated himself on that point to the Corinthians, and his word will bear repeating today. There is neither virtue nor vice in stage or screen as media, but there may be either vice or virtue in their content. Today the theater has in general a greater literary, artistic, and ideological integrity than have most of the products of Hollywood; and while its tradition allows of freer language and freer treatment than does the moving picture producers' code, its very frankness often is more healthy than is the half draped suggestiveness produced by a censorship which fears not dirt but only moronic conventionality.

Plays and films alike need to be carefully chosen if we are not to waste our time utterly; but they can be thus chosen. In so far as they are amusing, they refresh the spirit.

In so far as they are honest portrayals of life, they teach and challenge us. Sometimes the mood will call for a musical comedy, of which there are many that are unconditioned delight. Sometimes what we need is a waking up to reality; and many plays and a few films have it in them to stab the spirit broad awake.

Whether one can get to any considerable number of plays, or of operas or concerts, is rigidly conditioned by geography. Radio and TV, however, have turned the living room into a readily accessible theater or symphony hall. For myself, I've given up the trek to San Francisco for operas since the Metropolitan has been on the air on Saturday afternoons. I escape the socialite pressure in the lobbies, and I can hear the soprano the better for not being tempted to guess her weight. (How often, in my younger days, I sat with eyes firmly closed to the horrors of a Wagner stage set, preferring the music uncomplicated by visual discords.) At home, as away, selection is the condition to satisfaction; but, barring the commercials which are practically 100 per cent unendurable, there are enough good things on the air to use up all the time we can spare for looking and listening.

Older than radio, but magically new in its recent technical achievements, is the phonograph. Even a simple and inexpensive player produces remarkable tone quality from the hi-fi recordings, and the choice of distinguished music is phenomenally wide today as compared with the little there was in the days before LP. For the clergyman in particular there is now available a wealth of noble religious works, from medieval plainsong through Palestrina and Purcell, and then Bach and Händel, to Stravinsky and Milhaud and Poulenc. Some of these certainly are worth buying, and absorbing by playing them many times. Others may be borrowed from the growing number of record-lending services. All will have a secondary and practical virtue, too, if they can be used to hint to organist and choir-master that something verily can be done about dragging tempi and choral imprecision.

One of the professors in a famous divinity school has the finest private collection of jazz recordings that I know of. In this field as in many others I am a rank amateur, but I was able to introduce him to the "progressive jazz" of Dave Brubeck—who, by the way, is a very learned mu-sician, and a longtime student under Darius Milhaud both in Paris and on the Mills campus. Jazz has qualities that are worthy of investigation both as musical sounds and as expressions of our troubled and questing era. (I am not speaking of the saccharine sentimentalities of the popular love songs, which our informed adolescents rightly dis-miss as "sweet" and therefore "square.") The rhythms and harmonies of authentic jazz are shocking at first to the unaccustomed ear, as those of bop still are to mine; but they are intensely interesting to anyone who will listen, and in time they may become genuinely satisfying too.

Clubs and Lodges

Our age has ordered that man's social contact with his fellows shall be organized largely in and around clubs and lodges. From one point of view, these institutions are com-petitors with the church, and for all too many men they readily become substitutes. They are inadequate substitutes, for lodge theology is at best woefully incomplete, and luncheon-club benevolences are narrowly limited. Nevertheless a great many men find satisfaction in the men's special organizations, and they are not going to consider giving them up.

One reply that has been attempted, and in my observation with only dubious success, is to set up a church Brotherhood on the pattern of the service club. Several things are wrong here. One is that the church has its own institutional work to do, and that masculine horseplay is not integral to that work. A second is that, because the Rotary and Kiwanis and Lions have preëmpted the noon hours of the working week, the Brotherhood has to meet in the evening: so that the church is guilty of trying to take a man away from his family during those few hours of the day that he is free to be with his wife and children. A third is that the downtown club provides a variety of contact which scarcely is to be offered within the homogeneous and already well acquainted circles of the parish; that variety including, let us notice, the very important element of friendly association among members of widely variant religious groups.

Here I have to make a confession that would have surprised me greatly only two years ago. I had made many a luncheon-club speech, and I had been utterly snobbish about the whole setup. That sort of nonsense, I held, was not for me. Then one of the businessmen down on the corner spoke to me about joining the neighborhood Lions' Club. I agreed to visit it, without prejudice. I liked the fellows, and soon I found myself enjoying a new kind of fellowship. From November of 1953 I have maintained a perfect attendance record, because I have wanted to; and this means also that, by the make-up mechanism, I've had an amazing lot of new and happy contacts in districts and towns other than my own.

Participation as a man among men is value enough to

me to justify the expending thus of two hours a week, and the real friendships that have come to me are an added bonus. There are important by-products too; and not so much in the surprising fact that some of the men and their families turn up at an occasional college chapel service, as in the growing number of serious talks with chaps who have things on their minds and hearts that they long have been wanting to unburden without embarrassment. It no doubt is easy for a minister to become such a good Kiwanian that he may slight his obligations as a minister of Christ. I believe I have learned, on the other side, that the mission of the Christian ministry may be fulfilled in a very real way by one's being on occasion not the ex officio boss of a parochial Brotherhood, but a humble and participating member in a miscellaneous group of guys as ordinary as himself.

Holidays

The luncheon-club hours have to be counted as time off the job, and also as time "behind the scenes," because here the minister is to a large extent on all fours with the rest of the crowd. What other holidays may we allow ourselves, and what shall we do with them? Forty-six per cent of my Californians say they take a regular day off each week, and another 11 per cent have half a day. Monday of course is the favorite, Saturday a trailing second. The average annual vacation reported is two weeks and five days, with about 10 per cent expecting no recognized vacation at all.

"Trips" is by far the most common reply to the question, "What do you do with your vacation?" I suggest that that's a good answer also for the day or half-day that one fondly hopes he will be able to deduct from the working week.

Do as I say, not as I do. I was writing the first draft of this lecture on a Thursday, which is my one day without scheduled responsibilities on the campus. I gave up the morning to the writing job, not unwillingly, because I was eager to get the thing into shape. It was a beautiful spring day, and it promised a wonderful afternoon crossing the bay and walking in San Francisco—perhaps out by the ocean beach. At 10:30 A.M. the telephone rang, and so at four o'clock I sat in on an administrative conference. No afternoon off, and as a consequence the entire draft of this piece got written before the evening was done.

One can not afford this sort of thing all the time, and I promptly marked a huge "OUT" on my pad for the whole Thursday following. (Well, in the event I got half a day. It was St. Patrick's, and I walked lazily and happily through the Mission district of San Francisco, which is about as close to Dublin as one can get this side the Atlantic.) If essential advance work is under control, and if there is provision for getting emergency messages within a reasonably few hours, we surely are entitled to be anonymous and incommunicado for a little while once in seven days. The car owner can take his wife and smaller children for a drive over a favorite scenic road or a hitherto unfamiliar one. A movie and/or a dinner away from home (the lady can use some time off the job too) may be combined with the drive, or in bad weather may be substituted for it. Old friends may be looked up, though preferably not those with whom one has serious business to discuss.

Golf or tennis might be fitted in here, or even hunting or fishing. Those last usually are easier to handle in the longer reach of the annual vacation, if they can be managed without sacrificing the pleasure of the rest of the family, and if the seasons happen to work out aright. Thirty per cent

of my Californians are fishermen, and half as many are
hunters; but several of them indicate that their opportunities are rather few.

A holiday at home seems often to offer a tempting prospect. More often than not, I suspect, it turns out to be a
fraud. The habitual daily routine supervenes for both husband and wife, the youngsters are out for their regular playing with the neighbors' children, and the phone rings regularly with the regular sort of interruption. Again, of course,
absence requires advance coverage for emergency situa-
tions: the servant of the servants of God may not be out
of reach unless he leaves his people's sudden needs provided
for. If this is adequately done, the healthiest place for the
vacationer to be is away.

Some like to go to the same mountain or beach area
year after year, and some delight in new adventuring. Just
at present Mrs. Hedley and I are combining vacation time
with prospecting for a place to retire to. We've not yet
found one we can agree on; but we've seen a lot of gor-
geous scenery, we've met numbers of delightful people,
and we've had no end of fun. Come to think of it, what
better description of an ideal vacation could there be?

Hobbies

At home in the evenings, or on a programmed "day off"
when the weather seriously discourages adventuring out,
there should be room for the kind of self-entertainment
that is known as a "hobby." Among the California pastors
gardening is the favorite (of course we admit no weather
problems in our Golden State), with shopwork in wood or
metal second, and photography third. Golf and fishing are
tied for fourth in this category, as well as being listed among

the "active sports." Bird study has two devotees, and model railroading and antique model cars have a single *aficionado* each.

It would seem that stamp collecting has gone out of fashion, or perhaps has been relegated to the younger members of the family. Nevertheless I would put in a plug for philately as an ideal pursuit for relaxed and quiet winter evenings, and as one of the most educative of leisure-time activities. It doesn't have to be expensive, either. A fairly recent catalogue is essential, but an elaborate printed album isn't. Ruled graph paper from the dime store avoids all wasting of empty sheets, allows the collector's ingenuity and taste to plan his own independent arrangements, and never passes out of date. The beginner can buy a lot of miscellaneous stamps for very little money, but he doesn't absolutely have to buy any at all. Every minister's mail brings in a tremendous variety of American stamps even if no others, and knowledge that a collection is in the making is almost sure to produce donations in irregular batches but considerable quantity.

Geography, history, economics, all are abundantly illustrated and imperceptibly taught by the stamps that our nation and others have issued. She was no stamp collector, that horrifying Mills student who last winter asked, "Is Africa in South America?" The sequence of the British monarchs in this century is no puzzle to those who know the dates of the philatelic portraits of Victoria, the two Edwards, the two Georges, and Elizabeth II. The tragedy of the European inflation after World War I scarcely can be realized more sharply than through a study of multiplying face values in successive months. I have before me a picture frame which houses unused German stamps to the value of the total German national debt of 1921, eight hundred billion marks (or two hundred billion dollars at the prewar par), and which in 1942 cost me exactly ninety-five cents, including the California sales tax. If stamps don't seem interesting for one's self, they still might be considered as something to start a boy on. And one can very easily catch the contagion.

The photographer makes his pictures first, then persuades his friends to look at them. Here also the pursuit can be costly or almost costless. There is much satisfaction to be gained from taking a Brownie on a journey or a hike, and there is much to be learned about the effective composing of a picture from the actual and mostly immovable materials before one's eyes. There is, on the other hand, an almost infinite field for the development of technical aptitudes if one has sufficient time and money to become an expert operator behind the finder and in the dark room. The only caveat, apart from that of expense, is with reference to the friends who really may not care to spend a whole evening looking at Susie against successive backgrounds of trees, mountains, lakes, and motels.

The manual dexterity of the typical American is a continuing marvel to us whose origins were European. I admire my friends who can handle a shopsmith and turn out handsome and useful products for the home. Up to now I admire without venturing to emulate; but I do envy. The thrill of any kind of creation is one of life's great joys; and it is good for us, whose creations are mostly verbal, to produce sometimes in metal or in wood. This may effect real financial economy too, when skills are sufficiently developed and the product turns out to be a usable one. But here I am unqualified indeed, and I restrict myself to applauding from the outskirts of the crowd.

There is one form of manual activity in which recently

I have become involved, and with greater success than I had supposed possible. Because I was lucky enough to have a fair share of traveling in my younger days, I've always been fascinated by ships and trains. For long years my wife stood patiently by while I glued myself to shop windows and watched model railroads in operation. Ultimately she decided to put an end to my frustration, and gave me a $10 toy train for Christmas.

End of the game room downstairs. Today it is a town-and-country scene with five trains weaving around and through it, and over it on an elevated structure which is my first and only successful carpentry to date. But the playroom floor soon turned out to be too small and too flat, and I moved on to the unimproved part of the furnace room. Here is a magnificent mountain slope, with track winding by measured grades past oil refinery and ranch and lumber mill to a California mining town. At first I bought plastic kits for buildings, and then I graduated to cardboard and balsa ones. Next I learned that cardboard and balsa are available much more cheaply in their semiraw states. Soon I concluded that I wasn't incapable of a modicum of designing on my own account. Recently I've bought almost nothing, and I've built from my own plans with growing satisfaction and increasing success.

Not yet have I ventured to try making any of the operative equipment, but obviously that has to come next. Meanwhile I've learned more than I dreamed was possible for me about the vagaries of electric current, about engines and car types, about how to cut and fasten together and paint. My eyes have been newly opened too as I move about my home town or travel to distant places; and my oil tanks and water towers and housing units take on a new verisimilitude as increasingly I teach myself to estimate dimensions and to observe precise details of arrangement.

Trains, let us face it, are not a child's toy but a man's. The boy of course may be used as an excuse, and Christmas as a time to start. But his attention span is short, and his analysis of detail will not be sharply accurate for some years to come. The real fun of a model-railroad layout is reserved for one who sees the world discerningly, and who has learned to recreate it for himself accurately on a 1:96 scale. I believe I can claim that my trains have given pleasure to a number of people, young and old. That's velvet. What the trains have done for me is to sharpen my vision, to wake my imagination, to challenge my ingenuity, to teach me new skills; and not least, after a rugged day, to charm away the worries of tomorrow with a ruler, a razor blade, a jar of white glue, and a box of paints.

To those whose favorite hobbies I have left out of my listing, I humbly apologize. No one of us can go in for everything, nor can he know much that's significant about anything except at firsthand. If one's specialty employs his technical abilities, if it develops his capacities in any direction, if it opens his eyes to new vistas telescopic or microscopic, if it relaxes the tensions of the daily round, it makes him a better man. Let us extend our pitying condolences to that 9 per cent of the California padres who wrote "None" in reply to the hobby question.

Pets and Poultry

Those men are likely to counter that they have more important things to do than play trains or paste in stamps. They are pointing to the danger that inheres in any hobby: which is that it may prove so fascinating that it will absorb an undue proportion of time and energy, and thus may become not a refreshment but a besetting sin. This can be peculiarly and troublingly true when the hobby is the care and feeding of pets. Let me hasten to add that I have had four important dogs in my life (a Peke, a collie, a pointer, and a pit bull), and that the Hedley household at the moment includes two permanently resident cats—of which one is regularly in production. When I speak of pet problems, therefore, I do so not wholly without sympathy or knowledge.

Dogs and cats are supposed to be natural enemies, and dog men and cat ladies carry on a parallel war of their own. I shall discuss here no question of merit, but I do raise one of convenience. We had to give up on dogs finally, because our schedule simply didn't allow us to give to Diller's Queen of Clubs the continuing attention she demanded and deserved. In the country or in a small town, where a dog can range safely on his own, the pleasure may be worth the price. I question whether it can be for a professional man living on a city street.

Cats by contrast are self-managing and perfectly capable of being self-amusing. I own that I respect and like their independence, and I don't resent their bland indifference to our comings and goings. A cat can be left at home, and will be content if a friendly neighbor will see that it has food and drink. A dog can not be left thus, and not always is he welcome at motels even if he has learned not to get carsick on the way. The rule has to be that a pet is permissible if he doesn't prevent the prompt and complete doing of one's primary job. The problem is that the pet can not be held responsible for the sudden responsibilities he may throw upon his devoted owner-slave.

This brings up the question of poultry. It's tempting, of course, to try and save on the cost of eggs and occasional fryers; and the hens safely imprisoned in a back-yard enclosure would seem to constitute a minimum threat to family and professional stability. I may be fearfully prejudiced here, in view of some brief experiences and some longer observations of my own. I have to say that as pets, in my judgment, chickens are a fearful bore, that as a hobby they're likely to occasion more labor than enjoyment, and that as a commercial venture they have no place in the life of a man whose working time is dedicated wholly to the service of God.

Nor is the issue disposed of by turning the egg gathering and pen cleaning over to the wife and children. I've seen that tried too, and not to the glory of God nor to the happiness of his people. Poultry raising is a specialty for the specialists in poultry. I'm glad they are willing to take it on. I know it's no business of mine, and I suggest the making of a sober estimate as to how far it can be either a personal pleasure or a legitimate business for a busy minister of Christ.

All in the Family

A Presbyterian pastor in Oakland, who is a recognized expert on family relations and who is in continual demand for speeches on that subject, no longer accepts any public or social engagements for Friday evenings. He made that rule for himself after his son's school counselor reported the boy's own comment: "Dad is so busy making speeches on how to run a family that we never see him around the house." Whether it's family therapy or church activities or community betterment, the minister may find himself so boxed in by public appointments that his own wife and children get little of his private attention. This is a danger we all face, and one we must learn to guard against.

The California consensus on "Do you and your family take your recreation together?" was a rather disheartened and disheartening, "We try to." Some of the difficulty here is not the father's fault at all, but is the product of our present urbanized living. The typical city family has surrendered its educational functions to the school, its religious life to the church, its recreational activity to the playground, the movie, and the summer camp. Children play, and seem to want to play, in their own age groups rather than with their parents: and this especially in those critical ages of the seventh, eighth, and ninth grades. The dominant forces in the community tend on the whole to pull families apart rather than to bind them together.

It becomes the more necessary that we, who say we believe in the family as the principal social institution, shall find ways in which our own families still may operate as happy and creative social units. In my time as a paterfamilias (Mrs. Hedley and I are parents emeriti now), a special problem in the evenings was to train myself into a real interest in the game of Monopoly. I suppose today's equivalent would be Scrabble. The kids do love to play games with their parents, if they're given half a chance; and a little weariness with their small excitements, a little loss of time from solitarily silent reading, are minor prices to pay for the youngsters' satisfaction in finding that Father and Mother can be playmates as well as disciplinarians.

It is in sports that Pop may become a friend of his son on something like even terms. How the lad rejoices when he can go fishing with Dad, how he exults when at last he can play him equally at tennis, how proud he is of a father who doesn't muff the ball in a predinner game of catch! Going to a big game together is an extra special event, and Mother and the girls had better not be stuffy about it. If they will go along a few times, they'll learn for themselves the difference between a forward pass and an infield fly, and so they will find themselves full sharers in the family's delight over a home-town victory.

Hobbies too are opportunities for family sharing, even if the feminine share is but to respond pleasantly to the command for admiration. Often it's more than that (*c'est moi qui parle*): a new and bright idea, ever so innocently tossed out, which will require a total reorganization of the stamp collection or an entire regrading of the railroad track. One can even envisage the possibility of a girl's becoming an expert model builder in her own right. That needs to be watched, though, lest in compensation one finds himself being trained in how to knit a sweater for the dog.

Earlier I have mentioned the lost art of walking. Is it not time that we began to worry about the dying art of conversation? The breaking up of family meals into a staggered series of cafeteria snacks, the radio that blares while we are eating, the TV program that pulls us away from the table bearing our dessert and coffee with us: all these fashions of the time discourage anything like good, coherent talk.

Some of us were brought up on the rule that children should be seen, and not heard; but even though we were forbidden to interrupt, and were discouraged from chipping in, we did hear at breakfast and luncheon a certain amount of consecutive and relaxed discussion. Whether it was of cabbages or of kings mattered not. In either case we heard much of interest, and we also learned something of the manner in which civilized people exchange ideas.

This freer America of ours does not prohibit the child's

95

speaking, but it gives him little chance to speak to an appreciative family audience. The unfortunate habits of our schedules destroy equally one of the parents' best chances to share knowledge and opinion with their children. Both at mealtimes and in the living room afterward, one of the most pleasant of recreations can be a gabfest; but it is unpleasantly significant that the standard phrase for this is "a good, old-fashioned gabfest." We as preachers do a lot of solo talking to our congregations. How about some trio or quartet, or even choral, talking within our households? We might do just as good teaching, and the chances are that we'd manage quite a bit more learning.

Vacations offer this age's best chance to restore something of the old family solidarity. Away from home and familiar friends, those who know each other turn to each other for comradeship and self-confidence. This is one good argument for making the vacation a varied and wandering adventure, rather than a return each summer to the same standard locale with the same established neighbors. In that pattern the deleterious urban habits are all too likely to assert themselves: Father yarning with the men on the beach, Mother chatting with the women on the porch, youngsters spending their time with other youngsters goodness knows where.

I have not forgotten that our theme is "keeping in condition." Part of the necessary conditioning of the healthy spirit is ease and contentment and fulfillment in a relaxed and relaxing family life. Said a woman colleague of mine, "The trouble with a woman professor is that she doesn't have a wife to look after her." The trouble with a celibate priest is the same, and he loses far more in intimate sharing of life than he can possibly gain in privacy for his studies and freedom for his labors. Let us give thanks to God for our wives and children. Then let us show that our thanks are honest by being real participants with them in all that makes a family whole and its living complete.

Everything I have been saying rests upon the assumption that the minister is a man as other men are. (Yes, I am quoting Nick Bottom, who at the moment neither looked nor sounded like a man, but like a donkey.) To stay in condition for his special task, the clergyman requires exactly the same tonics for body, mind, and spirit that all the other men along the street do. He needs to keep his physique toned up, his senses alert, his energy sufficient to the many drains upon it. He has a special responsibility to be interested in, and to know about, the innumerable varied things that interest the folk among whom he lives and whom he is called to serve. He must find mechanisms for himself that will reduce tensions, and rest tired eyes, and recreate stamina.

Re-creation is precisely the requirement. Recreational life for the parson is less an escape from duty than it is a duty in itself. Resting happily and playing healthily, he will build his own health and happiness, and the well-being and joy of his parish as well. Keeping in condition is principally a behind-the-scenes matter, for the time on stage often is wearing and wearying. Behind the scenes, then, one of our principal duties is to keep ourselves fit for our job out front.

* * *

O HEAVENLY Father, who hast filled the world with beauty; open, we beseech thee, our eyes to behold thy gracious hand in all thy works; that, rejoicing in thy whole creation, we may learn to serve thee with gladness; for the sake of him by whom all things were made, thy Son, Jesus Christ our Lord. Amen.
—John Wallace Suter, Jr., A.D. 1917.

V

CHECKING THE CASH

Personal Finances

*ALMIGHTY God, Lord of heaven and earth, who
ever pourest forth thy blessings upon this land and on
us thy children; we who receive thy bounty give ever
our thanks unto thee in thy holy Church; through
Jesus Christ our Lord. Amen.*
　　　　　—Adapted from John Cosin, A.D. 1626.

*　　*　　*

President Lynn White, Jr., tells of a stately Scottish relative
of his who devised her own lengthening of the Shorter Cate-
chism. "What is the chief end of the law?" she asked. And
her ragged Glasgow urchins chorused eagerly in response,
"To confirm the rich in their riches, and to restrain the
vicious poor." On this basis it would seem that most of us in
the ministry are more likely to be restrained than con-
firmed; and even though we be innocent of viciousness, restraint surely is in order in our dealing with the little money
that does come into our possession.

Rightly or wrongly, the clergy commonly are suspected
of more than ordinary ineptitude in the handling of their
personal finances. Aside from the fact that we have an ad-
mittedly small margin to work on, we are thought to have
our heads so far in the clouds that we can't count the cash
in our pockets. Sometimes we are seen as chiselers, sometimes as spendthrifts. Our faults may not be quite as serious
as the charges would suggest; but the best way to meet the

charges is to be sure that we do make as much sense financially as our resources will allow. How ought we to spend? How to give? There are some specific guideposts we shall do well to heed.

Income

Annual clerical incomes in our California small-town survey ran from $2,400 to $6,360, with a median of $4,000 and an average of $3,953. Ninety-four per cent of the men were married, and they had an average of 2.42 children per family. Both the top and the bottom salaries went to older men whose children are grown up and away from home. The range for men with children under twenty-one was from $2,500 to $6,000. For these the median and average were somewhat higher, being $4,200 and $4,460 respectively.

Interestingly enough, a 1952 study reported in *Presbyterian Life* by Donald L. Hibbard showed an average salary of $4,495 for all Presbyterian ministers in the country, and a 1953 one by the Methodist Board of Pensions an average of $4,465 for all Methodists except students and supplies. Hibbard, assuming a sixty-hour working week, comes out at an hourly wage of $1.44. If we apply the same measurement to our last California statistic and to the Methodist one, we arrive at wages of $1.43. It would seem that the three surveys tend to validate one another.

A lower figure is shown in the 1953–1954 report of a large Methodist conference on the Pacific Coast. This shows that 344 charges paid to their pastors an average of $3,067 annually, or ninety-eight cents per hour for a sixty-hour week. Contributions from the conference board of missions added enough to bring the average annual salary to $3,272, and the corresponding hourly wage to $1.08. In another Far

Western conference, in the same year, the averages worked out at $3,565 and $1.15.

Using his sixty-hour calculation for the clergy, Hibbard shows their hourly wage as being appreciably below those which he cites for truck drivers, painters, carpenters, and electricians. Few of these, however, have been getting much overtime in the past few years. In terms of total income as a source for a year's expenditures, it probably will be fairer to use the forty-hour week as a measure: fairer, and revealing enough. This would give us hourly wages, for the northern Californians, the total of Methodists, the Presbyterians, and the two Western Methodist conferences, respectively, of $2.14, $2.15, $2.16, $1.62, and $1.72. Current rates for electricians, carpenters, painters, and truck drivers in the San Francisco Bay area are $3.05, $2.90, $2.87, and $2.40. (It should be noted that the painters' contract provides for only a thirty-five-hour week.)

In the week of this writing the national steel strike has been settled at a basic rate of $2.38 an hour. Copper-mine workers are striking for a figure just under $2.20. The base pay for our local transit drivers in Oakland has now been set at $1.98. It would seem that so far as annual cash income is concerned we are about in the class of the semiskilled workers in industry, and well below that of the skilled construction groups. The question of the relative amounts of necessary training is worth thinking about, but not in the present context. We do need to ask, however, whether we ministers have any concealed advantages or disadvantages as compared with these manual workers whose economic equals or inferiors we appear to be.

If the typical construction or industrial employee has any income at all other than his wages, it will come from his savings. If he is typical, those won't amount to much. Only rarely has he a chance to develop a sideline; and his opportunities for overtime are limited to periods of national emergency and of very occasional rush orders. Actually many construction men don't get much over two hundred days of work in the year, with two hundred and fifty as a practical maximum. This means that their annual income can be calculated with reasonable accuracy by multiplying together the basic hourly rate and the number of eight-hour days worked. For the highly paid and regularly employed electrician, for example, $3.05 \times 8 \times 250 = $6,300$, strikingly near the top salary within the California clergy group. On the same basis the bus driver's annual figure would be $3,960, or almost exactly the California ministers' average.

Undeniably the minister has the advantage in job security. A member of a Methodist conference is guaranteed an appointment of some sort, and practically every clergyman can budget his year's proposed expenditures in full confidence as to his year's income. For the construction worker, in contrast, a few weeks of bad weather can make all the difference between comfort and penury; and the recent "annual wage" agreements reflect, and seek to correct, the long-standing pattern of irregular work in the automobile industry. During World War II the retail clerks in San Francisco campaigned vigorously for a labor draft for defense plants, so that they might benefit by the temporarily high wages without losing their seniority on the lower-paid but steadier jobs in the stores. With an industrial manpower draft ruled out, the great majority of these men chose to stay in the small-pay posts that carried security with them.

In general the clerk, carpenter, and bus driver remain in these categories, and get only the marginal increases that come from inflationary trends and union pressures. The highly successful minister, on the other hand, moves into

Carl A. Rudisill Library
LENOIR RHYNE COLLEGE

brackets that the driver and the carpenter never may hope to attain unless there is a second gainfully employed person in the family. There are seven pastoral salaries of $6,500 or over in one of the Methodist conferences I have cited, and fourteen in the other, with a top of $10,000. Hibbard estimates that in the 1970's, if present trends continue, $7,500 plus manse will be fairly common among the Presbyterians.

The minister's stated salary, moreover, is only in rare cases his total professional income. Auto allowances, travel expenses, wedding fees, gifts in kind, clerical discounts, all help to swell his effective resources. Pulpit supply fees in "vacation" times are another possible factor, though perhaps not worth the loss of rest that they involve. Payments for articles, and book royalties, are available to a few. The perquisite problem, both economic and moral, is that usually "them as has gets": wedding fees being more numerous and averaging larger in the bigger churches, and profit from writing being commonly limited to the men with established reputations and correspondingly high salaries. I would suppose that 10 per cent over all would be a fair estimate of the amount above salary which the minister is likely to receive. The total still isn't very much for the vast majority of God's special company of workers.

Are these perquisites legitimate? It seems to me that there is no need to be oversensitive about the accepting of a wedding fee. The usual payment to the minister is much smaller than that to the florist, to say nothing of the caterer; and he is entitled to feel that he is at least as important as the flowers and the food. Baptisms and burials are something else again. My own rule is to hand baptismal fees over to the Chapel funds, and to return any proffered funeral check to the bereaved family. Whatever our individual needs, we scarcely ought to accept personal profit from the performing of these first and last rites of the Christian life.

Sidelines are permissible if they are parallel to the minister's principal labors, or are an outgrowth of them, and if they do not rob his parish of time that he ought to be spending directly in its service. Writing and occasional lecturing may fit in here. Commercial ventures, on the other hand, are at cross-purposes to ministerial duty, and are not to be justified in the case of a full-time pastoral appointment. Among improprieties of this sort I would list both the selling of insurance and the raising of livestock, to say nothing of being a high-pressure book agent.

A word may be said here anent the matter of the minister's handling of any church funds. By all odds the soundest policy is for him neither to touch the incoming cash nor to issue payments of any kind. Even his own discretionary fund, if he has one, should have the checks against it drawn by someone else. Thereby the pastor will be guarded at once from his own carelessness or inexactitude, and from any possible cavil on the part of members of the parish. In Presbyterian terminology, the "ruling elders" are responsible for the financial aspects of church life, and the "teaching elder" for the spiritual. It will make things easier for everyone concerned if this distinction is fully recognized and consistently maintained.

All in all, no minister is going to drive a solid gold Cadillac unless he happened to choose millionaire ancestors, or to marry a wife who had them. He is not, however, the pathetic pauper that sometimes he has been made out to be. The bus driver lives in fair comfort, and raises a healthy family. The typical minister is at least as well off, if not slightly better. He too can make a go of things if he manages his household economy with conscience and intelligence.

Taxes

We need to remember, though commonly we forget, that anyone's nominal salary in our time is appreciably larger than the actual amount of cash he is free to dispose of as he will. The income tax is a heavy drain upon every one of us, carpenter and clergyman alike. Under the existing federal law a family of husband, wife, and two children, receiving $4,000 a year, surrenders to the United States $245. A family of the same size with $6,000 of income pays a tax of $600. When the income increases to $10,000, the tax becomes $1,540. In California the state income tax is nothing for the $4,000 family, $11.54 for the $6,000, $51.86 for the $10,000.

These figures mean that our median ministers, and their parallels who drive the buses, start with something like $3,755 in buying power; and that the carpenters, along with the relatively well paid among the California pastors, have just under $5,390. (The $10,000 man especially needs to note his net figure, which is only $8,408.) The secular workers are paying also for social security and unemployment compensation, while the minister now has the option of making payments on the former. These deductions are in fact investments in the future, but at the moment we are likely to see them only as subtractions from our spending power.

Less readily visible than income taxes, but definitely reducing our capacity to buy, are the excise taxes now being levied by governmental units at almost every level. Federal "luxury" taxes add 10 per cent to the cost of many items. The gasoline taxes in California, state and federal, total eight cents on each gallon, or almost one-quarter of the money paid. In Oakland the state and city retail sales taxes combined add 4 per cent on practically every purchase except groceries; and within the dollar they may run much higher, the established breakdown providing for almost 7 per cent on a thirty-cent item.

Nor does the tax problem for the individual end here. He knows that he pays property taxes if he owns a house; but he doesn't always realize that he pays them also if he rents one, for then the tax is provided for in the rental charge. Similarly the price of everything we buy includes a factor to cover the tax costs of the seller; and, under standard commercial policy, also to give him his normal percentage of mark-up on the taxes as well as on his other business expenditures. (I understand, for example, that the recent retail price rise for whiskey in California is almost double the tax increase which occasioned it.)

There is little that the private citizen can hope to do about the total tax pattern. Nor would many of us want to give up those governmental services, in their myriad national and local kinds, which the tax receipts provide for us. What we do need first of all, and can have if we care to, is a clear comprehension of the facts in the case. We may not budget on $4,000 or $6,000, if those are our salaries, but on $3,755 and $5,390. If we are thinking of buying in Oakland that light foreign car which is advertised at "$1,595 *here!*" we ought to know that it will cost us $1,658.80, plus at least $150 more if we take a year to pay for it. If at the corner drugstore we want an electric clock marked $7.95, we're going to hand over $9.07 before we can take it home. In short, we have less money than we think, and things are more expensive than they seem.

In terms of public policy, everyone of relatively low income should realize the important difference to him between sales taxes and a graduated income tax. The income tax is founded on the principle of ability to pay, the rates ranging from 20 per cent at $2,000 (after exemptions and deductions) to 91 per cent at $200,000 and over. The sales tax is at a uniform percentage for every buyer, whatever his resources. This sounds fair enough, until one realizes that the increase of one's income by a hundred times means nothing like a hundred times as much spending for consumption purposes. The surplus over such expenditures goes into savings, which means investment, and is not subject to sales taxes at all. The consequence is that percentage-wise the little man contributes, in a sales tax, a much larger share of his income than does the big man.

An Oaklander with $4,000, who spends $1,000 a year on taxable commodities, pays 1 per cent of his income in retail sales taxes. A man with $20,000 who spends twice as much for similar goods is paying only .04 of 1 per cent. In the case of the income tax, however, assuming that each of these families has four members, the $4,000 man pays to the federal government an over-all 6 per cent of his income, but the $20,000 man contributes a little over 20 per cent.

Property taxes fall somewhere in between, but toward the undesirable side because, like the sales tax, they are based on outlays made rather than on capacity to pay. This is one reason why slum property commonly pays high returns as compared with average residential holdings. The slum owner feels no pressure to make improvements, and so suffers from no increase in assessments. Henry George's single-tax plan, which was based on land values as such and would have ignored the uses made of property, was designed thereby to encourage its full using. If we are looking for a "single tax," however, which in our time will be most nearly equitable for everyone, the graduated income tax is the evident answer.

Buying

We who have the lower incomes do use most of our money for buying, and we have to. Within the absolute limits of what we have available to spend, we can do well or badly in our purchasing. Three simple rules will help us toward establishing a favorable ratio between money expended and values received. They are: (1) buy carefully; (2) buy good stuff; (3) buy for cash.

Buying carefully is largely a matter of patient shopping. This may be the literal journeying from store to store, "just looking," which every woman loves and every man detests. It may be also, and for the man less painfully, the using of dependable information services such as those of Consumers' Research and Consumers' Union. What we need to find out before we buy anything, and what advertising does not tell us with any precision, is where to find the best quality at the lowest quoted price.

Because competition in general makes apparent prices much the same, whether for a loaf of bread or a television set, the qualitative factor is the one that chiefly must be investigated. At the same time there are price differences between types of stores, and sometimes even between basement and upstairs in a single store. Snob appeal permits accepted overcharges for many items, whether steaks in a fashionable restaurant or flowers from the "right" shop. To snob appeal the minister has no right to yield, either on principle or for purely practical reasons. His duty both to his job and to his family is to insist on commercial integrity by dealing only with those purveyors who maintain it.

This does not mean, however, that the least expensive item of its type is necessarily the best buy. "A poor man," remarked a wise old banker, "can't afford to buy cheap goods." Sleazy clothes at 50 per cent less than good ones are a poor investment, for they will last less than half as long. Thus also everything from dime-store toys to automobiles should be checked for durability even before one looks at the price tag; and the more carefully the less we can afford to spend.

Knowing that we have little cash on hand, we are readily tempted by charge accounts and installment plans. If we yield to them we certainly line up with the national majority. It does not follow that we are being wise. There are few of us who will admit to ourselves that we're not likely to have much more cash sixty days hence than we have now, or who can see that $57.50 a month is just as big as $1,035 a year and a half from today. (Actually it's a good $150 more, by the time one figures in carrying charges on the one hand and potential interest on the other.) The typical consequence of the casual approach to credit is serious overextension, with psychological strain at least and quite possibly with public disrepute as well.

The old heap will get us around the parish a while yet, and the drapes in the living room won't fall apart for another year. If we buy the new ones when we have the money, they'll be new then and will serve us that much longer; and we won't have fretted, and paid extra costs, and engaged in mutual recrimination within the family. As for the TV and the deep freeze, they can wait—and ought to—until we're in the luxury class. And if we never make that, we still can live happy, useful, and debt-free lives.

The same principles apply equally to grocery bills, gasoline credit cards, postpayable airplane flights, and all the other invitations to overspending that our age presses upon us. Paying for dead horses is a gloomy affair, and not paying for them gets us into trouble. Buying for cash, moreover, frees the buyer to unrestricted shopping for values wherever they may be. Every candidate for admission on trial into a Methodist conference is asked, "Are you in debt so as to interfere with your work?" Obviously the practice of inquiring on this point grew out of serious and recurring scandals. It is incumbent on us to see that we do nothing to create new ones.

Banking

All credit buying is simply borrowing. If one absolutely has to have a loan, the bank is the place to go for it. Bank interest rates are reasonable, and bank policies are decent. Nowadays most banks will lend up to 10 per cent of one's annual income, with installment payments spread over the year. This is enough to get that first car a young pastor must have to cover a scattered parish, and it is about the maximum that anyone ought to be spending before he earns it. (If he has to do a considerable amount of driving, he might investigate the car-lease arrangements that now are available. Some of our largest corporations have decided that these offer more economy than does outright purchase.)

"Personal loan" companies in general should be given a wide berth. To the careless their interest rates sound low, but "2 per cent a month" turns out to be 24 per cent a year. Some have followed the practice of making out the note for more than the amount loaned, with a "take it or leave it" ultimatum; and once the borrower has signed, he has no legal recourse because his signature itself is of the nature of perjury. When one becomes involved with operators of this sort, he will have a hard time trying to get out of their clutches. Whatever the need, the "loan company" way is a poor device for trying to meet it.

To lend money to the bank, by way of depositing in it, is a happier and healthier enterprise than is any borrowing. For people who are sailing close to the wind, the most convenient type of checking account is that which provides the checks in advance at ten to fifteen cents each, and involves no charge for a low balance as such. With this, if one keeps his stubs accurately recorded and calculated, he knows exactly what his balance is from day to day, and has to make no deductions when he gets his statement.

A second advantage of this arrangement is that it will permit two accounts, one each for husband and wife, without a penny of extra cost. Joint accounts, while romantically attractive in terms of sharing and mutual confidence, are extremely difficult to keep in balance and therefore are a common source of family disagreements. It should be remembered, too, that in many jurisdictions a joint account is frozen on the death of either signer, leaving the survivor temporarily without access to the funds.

Savings accounts are useful for short terms and relatively small amounts: as for example in putting away the money for Christmas gifts or for the summer vacation. Because of the low interest rate they are less than satisfactory for large sums or extended periods. Any amount over $100, say, which is not needed for early outlay, had better be withdrawn and put into something which will yield a higher return.

Giving

The first and most important type of investment for the Christian minister is that which he makes in the Kingdom of God. Probably there are few clergy, whether or not they make the formal calculation of a tithe, who put back less than 10 per cent of their incomes into the Christian enter-

prise. Small costs of goods and services for the church con-
tinually have to be paid out of pocket, and are not easy to
recover from the official funds. A certain amount of individual charity is almost inevitable, though one ought to
avoid getting a general reputation as an easy mark. Nor can
one remain forever heedless of the outstretched palms of
his college and seminary alumni offices.

Along with occasional giving of these kinds, the pastor
will book himself and his family for regular payments toward the church budget, both because he will want to and
because he will be setting a useful example. Some men have
thought it well to make their personal pledges entirely to
benevolences rather than to current expenses, so that their
giving will not be toward their own salaries. This probably
makes little difference in the long run, for experience shows
that most "designated gifts" turn out in fact to aid the
general funds of the given institution by relaxing the financial pressures at "undesignated" points.

In most towns there will be also the Community Chest or
its equivalent, in which as a good citizen the minister will
feel impelled to have a share; and every year there are the
Red Cross, the March of Dimes, and the Christmas seal cam-
paigns. There has to be a limit on donations, however. The
total amount one can reasonably give to all good causes
should be thoughtfully budgeted at the year's beginning,
with a portion set aside for emergency appeals of which one
has no advance knowledge. When that is expended, the
solicitor or cookie seller will have to be graciously turned
away.

Insurance

Because we live in a money economy, we must meet its
terms in the way of provision both for the foreseeable future

and for unforeseen eventualities. Investment is for the former, insurance for the latter, and the two ought not to be confused. What kinds of insurance ought one to carry, and in what amounts?

The size of a life-insurance policy will depend both upon available premium resources and upon the extent of family need that would ensue upon the death of the insured. Term policies, which cover only the premium periods and pile up no reserve credits, are the least expensive and therefore give the largest insurance coverage in proportion to outlay: typically more than twice as much as "straight life," and some seven times as much as "twenty-year endowment." The more elaborate types of policies commonly are urged as investments; but they are not good investments as such, because inevitably they divide the profit between the in- surance company and the insuree. As long as there is enough term coverage to provide for sudden death, any accumula- tions intended for the children's education, for retirement, and so on, are better placed in one or another of the direct investments discussed hereinafter.

Health and accident insurance is mandatory in our time for people in the lower brackets. Even though one never collects, the mental peace of knowing that a sudden illness will not devastate the family's resources is well worth the making of the payments. Where clinic plans are available, they commonly will be found to give the greatest protection at the smallest cost. All medical-insurance policies, however, should be read very carefully in advance of purchase, for some of them list so many exceptions that their benefits may turn out to be largely unavailable.

The automobile owner will need to insure his car, but still more the other driver's car and the other man's life. Collision insurance at $50 deductible costs almost twice as much as at $100 deductible, which at typical current rates means that the $50 difference would be used up in two years' payments. Property damage and public liability protection is essential, and in amounts as large as one reasonably can afford. Whether or not the car is owned by the church, the possibility of suits brought against it because of use in its service make it advisable that the policy should read "John Jones and the First Methodist Church of Plainville."

Fire insurance is relatively cheap, and worth having for one's books and personal property whether or not one owns the house in which they are. The insurance carrier should be notified immediately in the case of a change of location, and the appropriate adjustments made. Theft insurance has less of meaning for most of us, inasmuch as we have few possessions that would interest a burglar. Tornado and earthquake policies are relevant according to region, and only for building owners. The ruling principle in all insurance buying is to estimate not what one thinks he can afford in premiums, but what he cannot afford in the event of the particular misfortune being considered.

Investments

For the first years of one's ministry buying, giving, and minimum insurance coverage are going to use up so much of the total income that any question of investments may seem purely academic. Even so, it is possible, by careful planning and firm self-discipline, to place some small and recurring amounts under guard for future reference. As one's salary goes up through the years, the proportion of saving (not only the absolute amount) ought steadily to increase.

Pension funds of course are savings, and happily they are

nowadays inescapable for the clergy of most major denomi-nations. The added pension of the federal old-age and survivors' insurance, at long last made available to us, ought by all means to be accepted immediately and the payments maintained faithfully. The great virtue of the social security scheme is precisely that it is not actuarial, but political; which means that the amount of benefits will continue to be increased by the Congress in proportion to increases in the cost of living. The likelihood is, therefore, that the ultimate money value will be greater than could be secured by any purely mathematical and financial arrangement.

A sample list of current pension claims in one great Church shows that only the men with more than twenty-two years of service are receiving as much as the $80 monthly of the federal plan. This means that social security would have more than doubled the retirement resources of all who served a shorter time; and it would have raised the in-come of the most highly pensioned of these men, one whose active ministry covered almost forty-nine years, by just about 50 per cent. It is sad that such benefits are not available to these gallant veterans. It will be stupid on our part if we fail to take advantage of our better fortune.

The amounts we pay into pensions and social security are specified and limited. Any further reserve funds we may have available can go into investments of many kinds, wise or foolish, profitable or disastrous. The general rule is that safety is coupled with fairly low returns, and potentially high profits with serious risk. (Even the horse-racing charts show this, but of course no clerical reader would understand them.)

Bonds represent direct loans to an enterprise, govern-mental or private, at fixed rates of interest. They are first charges upon the funds, and theoretically carry no participation in management's fluctuations of gain and loss. The interest on the standard government savings bond works out at 3⅓ per cent a year on the initial investment, and therefore at decreasing rates as the interest accrues, so that over the ten-year period the average is 2.9 per cent. The combination of security and low return holds bond prices relatively steady, with usually a slight upturn when the stock market becomes shaky. The average price of forty standard bonds on 30 June 1955 differed by less than .02 of 1 per cent from that of 30 June 1950, and their average rate of return was about 3 per cent.

Buying stocks as investments and "playing the stock market" are two entirely different things. The former is purchase for a long time, the latter a matter of quick buying and selling on the basis of guessing about immediate trends in prices. Income from stock dividends is a proper return for supplying funds for the company's use. Income from profits on stock sales is nearer to gambling; and for the busy minister the attempt to secure it is likely to be financially dangerous as well as ethically dubious.

A long-term rise in stock values, however, is a sign of a prospering economy; and a stock which has appreciated steadily is comparable to a city lot which has gained in worth because of a growing population. The interval from 1950 to 1955 shows sixty-five selected stocks averaging today more than twice the quotations of five years ago. This means that, apart from dividends received, the 1950 investor has doubled the amount of his investment without paying out any additional money. Correlatively, however, he ought to remember that a serious recession might mean his losing as much or more without getting any cash.

Among stocks, those of utility companies are the most dependable and the least exciting, while those of industrial concerns stand in contrast at both points. The rise in utility stock prices over the five-year period has been just over 50 per cent, and that in industrials almost 120 per cent. In case of a business slump, again, utility prices and utility dividends will drop much less sharply than will their industrial counterparts, for the reason that the demand for gas and electricity is more constant than is that for automobiles and household appliances.

The small investor is likely to do best by entrusting his buying to an investment pool. These are handled, for quite reasonable operating fees, by informed agents who spread the total investment widely and make continuing adjustments to the shifting market situation. It is possible to buy such trust shares with an initial deposit of as little as $40. The consistent adding of an equal amount monthly will pile up capital and interest at a quite surprising rate.

The pension plan in force at Mills College permits one to assign 50 per cent of his monthly deductions, and of the College's equal contribution, to a scheme of this kind, so as to provide ultimate returns not at the nominal money value of the premiums but at the actual level of values in future years. It may be worth recording that all the members of our Mills Department of Sociology and Economics, and no one else on the campus, elected thus to use the full 50 per cent when the plan first went into effect. I will say also that no one of us has regretted it yet, for after only three years the present value accumulated is 21 per cent above the premiums paid.

If there are no surviving children, nor other persons or causes to which one strongly desires to leave money, the purchase of annuities may be the soundest investment of all for man and wife. The annuity brings principal and interest together in a kind of reversed life insurance, in which

the financial institution is betting that the buyer will die
and the buyer that he won't. The annual receipts from annuities are by their nature much larger than those from
dividends as such, for they are designed approximately to
amortize the total investment within the lifetime of the investor. A further advantage for the minister is that since his
own life expectancy is higher than the general average, he
is likely to secure longer than average payments from the
buying of a standard annuity.

What of real estate as investment? For retirement it may
be desirable to buy a house well ahead of time, and to use
rental receipts against the purchase price. This will ensure
having a place to live in, and ideally with minimal costs at
a time when income is sharply decreased. An even better
deal is offered by some church agencies in a "Life Lease"
arrangement, essentially similar to an annuity, in which
the costs are not those of total purchase but only of the use
of the property during the lifetimes of the people concerned.
Savings here are likely to be $15 to $20 monthly as compared with the expense of an ordinary buying arrangement.

On the other hand, investment real estate as such is difficult for the private person to handle. Tenants are not always
dependable, and there are recurring bills for repairs and
replacements as well as the continuing ones for taxes and
maintenance. The minister has no time to be an active
business enterpriser, and he is unlikely to make much from
real-estate holdings if he has to hire someone else to do
the managing. Of course, if land values go up decisively the
owner may make a substantial capital gain by selling; but
if he is well enough informed to be sure of doing this he
scarcely has been devoting his full attention to the work of
the ministry.

Real Wages

All that I have been saying rests upon an assumption that ought now to be made explicit. It is that a dollar isn't a dollar, but a highly volatile symbol of our economic ups and downs. One way of stating it is that a dollar was worth ten loaves of bread when I was young, but is worth only four today. It follows that a dollar saved will be less or more than a dollar earned, as the economy in general waxes or wanes.

The total historical trend is inflationary, despite the rigors of occasional depression. This means that fixed money savings, indicated by specific figures on a sheet of paper, are likely to mean less when we come to spend them than they did when we restrained ourselves from spending. Savings accounts, life-insurance policies, bond purchases, all are of this type, for they remain at their original nominal values. The social-security plan and the investment trusts, on the contrary, will reflect the general changes in the economic scene, and therefore give promise of doing more toward meeting our actual needs at the price levels of tomorrow.

At the moment it seems that the crest of the current commodity price curve has been passed, though one can not be sure of the impact of the most recent round of wage increases. As compared with 1950, an index of wholesale prices today shows an actual decrease of more than 1 per cent. If we set this beside the apparently healthy state of the security markets, we may hope that sound investment will give us in the long run an even greater advantage in buying power than the equality which would go with a generally rising price line. A healthy economy should be able to achieve such a gain of values over costs because of

118

steadily increasing efficiency in production. There is nothing against our sharing intelligently in such an economy's development, and also happily in its proceeds.

The ultimately real wages of the man of God are not in dollars, inflated or deflated, but in duty done. He has thereby a great advantage over the men of money in his attitude toward money itself, for he is neither overimpressed by its presence nor unduly distressed by its absence. "Money," observed Dr. Roy Wilson in his letter to me about an early draft of this present inquiry,

is the symbol of time spent, of life expended. Ours is the task properly to distribute the symbol: meeting our current creature needs, putting some of the energy of our life behind good causes, placing excess energy aside to meet that time when we no longer will be physically capable of making provision for current demands.

The minister owes it to himself, his family, his church, and his community, to know exactly how much of this "frozen energy" he has and to apportion it sensibly and constructively. He has to be exacting in self-discipline, but he can afford to be contentedly detached in mood.

Our salaries are but conveniences to make our service possible. Wise buying, creative giving, intelligent saving, all will help to make that service better by freeing us from financial worries and thereby releasing our full energies to the doing of our work. Money may not be our master, but it can be so handled that it will be a worthy servant. Never an end for us whose treasures are laid up in heaven, it yet may be a means toward our usefulness on earth. If we are good and faithful stewards of our own possessions, we shall be the better qualified as stewards of the mysteries of God.

* * *

ALMIGHTY God, our gracious heavenly Father; deliver us, we beseech thee, from the service of mammon, that we may do the work which thou givest us to do, in truth, in beauty, and in righteousness, with singleness of heart as thy servants, and to the benefit of our fellow men; for the sake of him who came among us as one that serveth, thy Son Jesus Christ our Lord. Amen.

—Abridged from Frederic Dan Huntington,
A.D. 1819–1904.

VI

STAYING IN CHARACTER

Devotional Life

> *O MOST loving Father, who willest us to give
> thanks for all things, to dread nothing but the loss
> of thee, and to cast all our care on thee, who carest
> for us; preserve us from faithless fears and worldly
> anxieties, and grant that no clouds of this mortal life
> may hide from us the light of that love which is im-
> mortal, and which thou hast manifested unto us in
> thy Son, Jesus Christ our Lord. Amen.*
> —William Bright, A.D. 1861.

* * *

The Greeks had a word for it. *Hypokrites,* whence our
"hypocrite," referred precisely to one who played a part
upon the stage. This brings us to the point of absolute
difference between the profession of the theater and that
of the church. An actor is not expected to remain in character once he is out of sight of the audience. His hypocrisy is
integral to his work, and a competent actor is one who can
play many different parts with an equal effect of reality. The
minister has one part only, though it is a complicated one.
He may not perform that part hypocritically, or he is no
minister of the Christ.

From time to time, indeed, the parson does need to relax.
As we have observed, he may do this by assuming for the
moment the guise of gardener or hunter or mechanic or
Rotarian. These are wholly superficial appearances, however, whose external activities may not be allowed to affect

at all the inner unity and continuity of the single character that belongs to the profession.

The relative difficulty of the time factor therefore is great. There is here no mere matter of ninety minutes a night in view of the playgoers. Before the people for almost forty hours in the week, the man of God is always before his God. Moreover, the rôle of the minister, rightly enacted, is likely to bring from the public quite as much abuse as it does applause. Standing for the absolutes of truth and justice and mercy, the Christian clergyman finds himself in a world where truth is at a discount, justice all too often on the bargain counter, and mercy tossed upon the rubbish heap. Being as human as we are, we find approval encouraging; and we rightly are encouraged by it, if we have won it without surrendering our values. Being human, we are inevitably hurt by disapproval. Our only means, then, to maintain our values is the developing of an inner strength sufficient to counter all the slings and arrows of what we regard as an outrageous opposition.

The Christian demand makes this yet the harder, by its insistence that such a strength may not be angry, may not be mere combativeness, may not be bolstered by self-love or by contempt of any man of those who dare oppose us. It is easy enough to love the lovable, and to show mercy to the grateful. What we are called to do is unceasingly to love the hateful, to be merciful toward those who have no mercy on us. We continue to be human, and we are required to live the divine life among devilish men. How may this impossibility become real in us?

The answer is devotion. The verb "to devote" often is reflexive, and with us it always must be. We devote ourselves. By an irrevocable vow we have given ourselves to this most difficult of tasks, have committed ourselves to this most demanding of lives. In the long experience of mankind it has become apparent that such total devotion hardly can be maintained without specific practices designed to preserve and to strengthen the total intent. Thus the act of devotion is performed by the devoted person, and the plural form "devotions" appears in support of the all-including singular. How can the minister manage to stay continuously in character? He will not do so save as he lives the devotional life.

Times and Places of Devotion

In what shall his devotional living consist? "Pray without ceasing" is a compelling injunction, to which we shall return before this present inquiry ends. Yet we scarcely shall pray all of the time, and while we are doing other things, unless we pray some of the time while we are doing nothing else at all. The men in California indicate an average of thirty-two minutes a day devoted to private devotion, plus fifteen minutes that are given to family worship. The range for the family is from five minutes to sixty, and for the individual from five minutes to two hours.

One virtue of family living seems to be pointed to by the fact that there is no sign of the bachelors' spending any more time in the solitary worship of God than the married men do. That is to say, the very existence of the parsonage family apparently leads the official tenant to set aside more total time for the conscious worshiping of God than do his celibate brothers. Leafing through the answered questionnaires as I write, I find that the maximum one hour for the family and two hours for the individual have been reported by the same man, a minister of the Church of the Nazarene. This turns out to be a man who finds time also to write out his sermon scripts in full, and to read the Bible for eight hours a week. Here surely is one who illustrates the bond between devotions and devotion.

In response to the query as to where private devotions occur, the dominant (and to me surprising) reply is the church office. The home is mentioned just over half as often, and the church itself by less than a third of the respondents. Only 11 per cent refer to that favorite of the church-avoiding layman, "out of doors."

The office perhaps does afford a surer privacy than does the household, if there happens to be a secretary to guard the door. Devotions here, however, scarcely can either begin or end the whole day; and not many offices have the décor or the atmosphere best calculated to stimulate the worshipful mood. Somehow I find it a bit difficult to see those men engaged in deep communion with God before desks loaded with papers and gadgets, and with themselves settled solidly in their broadbeamed swivel chairs.

The failure to worship privately in the place designed for public worship, admitted by more than 70 per cent of those who regularly lead their people's worshiping there, seems to me appalling. Presumably it reflects our long-standing misapprehension of what the house of God is for. So long as we think of the church as being primarily a place for the delivery of speeches, of course we won't use it when we can't round up an audience. When we learn to know the church as the place specially dedicated to be God's dwelling, and the one in which men and women habitually seek God and often have found him, we shall understand that God is no less available there to a single seeking soul than he is to a multitude.

Where better shall one pray than before God's altar? For the minister, this is the place where regularly he is privileged to seek to lead the people into the reality of the divine presence. Will he not want to prepare himself, humbly and faithfully and patiently, in that same place when no man is looking on? To fail to do this, to fail even to think of doing it, is to say pretty clearly that the Sunday service is an occasional public performance rather than the expression of an unending commitment. Let us return to the altar, penitent souls ourselves for our own thoughtlessness. It may be that then we shall be the better qualified to invite others to join us there.

At this point I cannot refrain from making a comment on the posture of prayer. We Methodist parsons used to kneel, and so did our congregations. Through the years, however, the concept of the church as auditorium made kneeling in public worship physically inconvenient, what with the slanting of the floor and the crowding together of the pews. Then the minister fell into the habit of standing to pray, while the people just sat: he presumably to be the better seen and heard, they merely to avoid exertion.

I humbly suggest that the minister need not be seen when he is praying, and while the congregation is supposed to be praying too. No one but God should be seen then. If kneeling is physically difficult for us because of long habituation against it, maybe reverence is spiritually difficult for us for the same reason. If we are embarrassed to kneel, perhaps we are embarrassed likewise to come into the presence of God; and in view of the common casualness of our approach to him we have every reason to be embarrassed.

So long as we are in the body, we may not think to separate the inward and spiritual grace from the outward and visible symbols. To seek God while sitting down seems to me to announce and to invite inattention and disrespect, whether on the part of the congregation in the pews or of the solitary cleric in his office chair.

Daniel symbolized his devotion by kneeling upon his knees three times a day, with the windows of his chamber opened toward Jerusalem. Our sacred shrine is nearer far, and not yet has it been desecrated by the alien hordes. It is full time for us to turn to it afresh, and within its hallowed walls to consecrate ourselves anew: humbling ourselves there before our heavenly King, offering ourselves to render our spiritual service, kneeling meekly upon our knees in token of our reverence to our blessed and only Potentate.

The Order of Private Worship

Kneeling in contrition before the altar, how may we open the way for God to speak to us? The effectual fervent prayers of a righteous man will find much of their own expression, and whatever prayer he offers in sincerity of heart is valid praying. Even the heart needs guidance, however, and the mind as surely needs discipline. Our faith is not one which we as individuals invented *de novo,* and our praying is incomplete if it fails of direction from the praying voice of all the Christian centuries.

Every Roman priest is required to say the Mass daily, and the clergy of the Church of England are supposed to make Morning and Evening Prayer what the prayer book calls them, daily offices. Such repetition of course can be debased into mere gabble: though scarcely more so than often is the Lord's Prayer, the one vestigial remnant of the old way that survives in many Protestant circles. I venture to propose a self-imposed rule like the Roman or Anglican one, just as an experiment: the daily discipline of following through the regular service of the Church, for the inner edifying of the single worshiper. I believe I am more than guessing when I suggest that he who tries this for a month will not lightly wish to give it up when the trial period has ended.

The majority of our churches now have worship books not only set forth by authority, but also rich in spiritual guidance. The authority still is commonly ignored in our public services, and so, alas! is the guidance in our private living. The Methodist who steeps himself in *The Book of Worship* will come closer not only to John Wesley, but also to John Wesley's God and his own. The Presbyterian who learns to use his *Book of Common Worship* will be the better qualified to glorify God and for ever to enjoy him. The Congregationalist who gets acquainted with the *Book of Worship for Free Churches* will discover therein that his freedom need not make him a separatist from the great tradition. The Disciple who apprentices himself to G. Edwin Osborn will realize with him that the truth of the Scriptures has been set forth not only in the canons of the Old and New Testaments, but that it breaks forth ever and again in the meditations of the disciples of Christ throughout the centuries.

The repeating of a single prescribed form day after day may produce boredom for the unreflective, but it provides rich experience for those whose spirits are awake to receive ever new light from the ancient and meaning-packed forms. From one to seven times a week it is my high privilege to celebrate the Holy Communion in our campus fellowship at Mills. Except for a few prayers, and the Epistle and Gospel, the words are always exactly the same. Not yet have I read them twice in the same way, for not yet have they failed to give me new and fuller meaning at one point or another. The same is true of every well ordered, devoutly written form of devotion. Let us not set aside the noble heritage which our several churches have committed into our hands for the enrichment not only of the public service but also of the individual spirit.

At the same time, private devotion allows to the individual a freedom of quest greater than is possible when many are seeking to pray together. A first means to the using of this freedom is for us to familiarize ourselves with the worship materials that have grown up in churches other than our own. *The Book of Common Prayer,* as the fountainhead of practically all the existing orders of service in English-speaking Protestantism, is an essential for every minister's library, and a continuing challenge to his own praying. Behind the English prayer book stand the ancient liturgies, both Eastern and Western. It is well for us to remember that Archbishop Cranmer did not appropriate all that was good in these, and it will be profitable for us to do our own adventuring within them. The Eastern Church has much to teach us of the quest and the experience of the Holy Ghost, and the Roman of the meaning of total dedication to the cause of our God and of his Christ.

Even older in their origins, but more recent in much of their present content and arrangement, are the prayer books of Judaism. The study of these will illumine the backgrounds of our own usages, and will add to our stock of known and available worship resources. In particular, the prayers of our Jewish brothers will help us to remember what the primary business of our praying ought to be. Very little of petition appears in the prayers of the synagogue, but very much of God's praise and not less of man's self-commitment. We Christians would pray better if we established something like the same proportion.

The Lutheran service books are little known outside Lutheran circles, no doubt because Lutheranism in America has been till recently so much a reflection of particular national backgrounds. These books will inform us generously not only as to Luther's special emphases, but also as to the extent to which he maintained the ancient Christian ways, and the intensity with which he held to the eternal Christian convictions. Every Methodist ought to know, and to use for the broadening of his Christian realization, the Presbyterian service book also, and the Congregational, and the Disciples'. So should the Disciple know and use the Congregational and Presbyterian and Methodist volumes, and all the way around the circle.

By such means as these, the man kneeling alone at his church's altar is not alone any more. The goodly fellowship of the prophets, the glorious company of the apostles, the noble army of martyrs, the holy Church throughout all the world, all are there with him, praising and acknowledging the one Lord of them all. In this unseen but unmistakable communion of the saints God is in the midst, and the glory of his countenance becomes ever the more gloriously revealed. Let us pray then with the church in the church, and our physical solitude itself will be turned into a triumphant spiritual fellowship.

Another means toward a worship that is in effect "behind the scenes" is to attend services in which one is not an official participant, but is in a pew among the laity. Only 37 per cent of the California pastors say that they make frequent use of this type of personal devotion. There no doubt are difficulties about achieving it in a small town with the Sunday-only pattern, where practically all services occur simultaneously. There also is the temptation to the professional, seeing another professional in action, to pay critical attention to the other man's techniques instead of to the state of his own soul.

Nevertheless, whenever it may be practicable for one to

share in the service without carrying the burden of responsibility for its effectiveness as a whole and its smoothness in every particular, the entry into the layman's rôle can be of important meaning to the cleric. To consecrate the Communion elements is a high privilege, and always a means at once to the celebrant's heart-searching and to his spiritual exaltation. To receive the consecrated bread and wine from another hand, kneeling rather than standing and silent instead of speaking, is an experience altogether different but not less vital. To be off duty for the nonce as a clergyman may mean to be very much on duty as a humble Christian believer. To be one unit of the company at the altar may be to become newly aware of one's participating membership in the universal household of the faith. The experiment is worth trying, and worth making available to our fellows of the cloth in brotherly mutuality.

Aids to Devotion

Spirit is not separable from mind, and meditation ever has accompanied devotion. In all the centuries the devout could not but set down the fruits of their thinking of the thoughts of God after him. What is called "devotional literature" then, as distinct from that which is planned consciously for the general and formal acts of worship, is another available and constructive aid to our spiritual conditioning.

The list is well-nigh endless, and each man will choose from it his own. Here I can do no more than mention some works which have meant so much to me that I am persuaded they will have value also for others. This judgment is supported by the fact that my list is an extremely conventional one; which means that already, and long before our time, it had secured the support of the Christian consensus.

The Bible stands first, and the reading of the Bible is not to be skimped in favor of anything else. As I tried to suggest in the first lecture, however, the Bible is not the only treasure house that we have to draw upon. God has not been silent, nor have his faithful people, through the eighteen centuries since the completion of the Scriptural canon. Let us journey quickly down through those centuries, pausing now and then to hear God and his people speak to the waiting heart of every century.

The Church in its beginnings was oppressed by the state and suspected by the public majority, and therefore many of its earliest writings were defensive in mood and polemic in tone. The spirit of devotion certainly was not lacking in men who died for their faith, but the spirit of debate inevitably appeared in their utterance. Only when the Church was secure in its position, and had been so for two generations, was the time ripe for the appearance of the first great classic of personalized Christian devotion. I urged earlier that we ought to read more of St. Augustine than his *Confessions*. This does not mean that the *Confessions* are to be ignored.

He who reads them will realize at once that he has not given up reading the Bible. I count seven Biblical quotations and allusions on the first page of my English copy, three on page 100, seven again on page 200, and eight on the half-page which brings the work to a close. St. Augustine thus is a worthy example to us as to knowing and absorbing the Scriptures. He is also a worthy contributor in his own right, daring us to be comparably honest about our sins, warning us against our self-satisfaction, encouraging us to find with him the everlasting love of the eternal God. "Our hearts are restless until they find their rest in thee." Ours it is to seek and find, with the busy Bishop of Hippo, the peace which God alone can give.

"St. Bernard" (of Clairvaux), observes an unnamed writer in the thoroughly secular *Columbia Encyclopedia,* "is one of the few saints of the medieval Church whom most later Christians delight to honor." The reason is evident in St. Bernard's work, of which we ought to know more than the beloved "Jesus, the very thought of thee," which indeed may not be from his hand. Unfortunately, not much of Bernard's certainly authentic writing is available in English translation, and almost none in the devotional anthologies with which I happen to be familiar. His *De Diligendo Deo,* however, a small work which might be described as a treatise of systematic mysticism, was newly translated in 1950 by an Anglican nun in England. Brief as it is, it is a compelling account of "that eternal longing, never satisfied, that knows no want," and which becomes "that fourth degree of love, when God is loved supremely and alone; for we no longer love ourselves save for his sake."

By no means so notable a figure as St. Bernard in his own time, but far better known to us, is Thomas à Kempis, whose actual name was Thomas Hammerken or Hammerlein. *The Imitation of Christ* may now with security be attributed to him in person. A later monk, it is said, set himself to underline the important passages in the *Imitatio Christi,* and wound up by thus marking the entire work. Our judgment is likely to coincide with his. I used the blindfold, pencil-stabbing device as I was writing this paragraph, and here are the three passages I hit upon:

Sometimes it is needful . . . manfully to strive against the sensual appetite, and not to consider what the flesh may or may not will; but rather to strive after this, that it may become subject, however unwillingly, to the spirit.

Again, "I have been taught by my loss, and O that I may prove more careful and not foolish thereby." And yet again,

Thou art the end of all good, and the fulness of Life, and the soul of eloquence; and to hope in Thee above all things is the strongest solace of thy servants.

Devotion does not exclude realism. Let us learn to profit by, and to share, the realistic devotion of this monkish copyist of five hundred years ago.

It was another Augustinian friar, a hundred years later, who changed the face of Western European Christianity. Martin Luther did not change its essence, however, and the epigrams in his *Table Talk* exhibit the same union of complete commitment with perfect practicality; for, as he says, "this natural life is a little piece of the life everlasting." On the same page is the needed counsel to the eloquent parson, "Faith has regard to the Word, and not to the Preacher"; and overleaf the heartening assurance and commission, "We lose nothing by the Gospel, therefore we should venture upon it all that we have." The Methodist will remember that it was during the reading of Luther's preface to the Epistle to the Romans, that evening in Aldersgate Street in 1738, that John Wesley felt his heart "strangely warmed." There still is warmth for us, and training too, in the works of him who made of the first Methodist a Lutheran as well as an Anglican.

At least two Roman Catholics of the sixteenth century, a Spaniard and a Savoyard, have much yet to say to modern Protestants. St. John of the Cross, a would-be reformer within the Church, is generally reputed to be abstruse and difficult. He was clear enough, however, when under official attack he could write,

To endure all things with an equable and peaceable mind, not only brings with it many blessings to the soul, but also enables us, in the midst of our difficulties, to have a clear judgment about them, and to minister the fitting remedy for them.

Nor is it hard for us to understand, though it may be extremely difficult for us to carry out, this injunction to Christian selflessness in its final purity:

He who acts out of the pure love of God, not only does he not perform his actions to be seen of men, but does not do them even that God may know of them. Such an one, if he thought it possible that his good works might escape the eye of God, would still perform them with the same joy, and in the same pureness of love.

It would seem improbable that St. Francis de Sales, a younger contemporary and an important ecclesiastic, and separated from St. John of the Cross by all the distance from Geneva to Ávila, had any direct knowledge of the elder mystic's writings. Nevertheless the two men had the same understanding of the irrelevance of any kind of result to the central Christian motive. Says St. Francis:

If we do not feel we are making progress or advancement of our hearts in devotion, such as we would wish, do not let us be troubled, let us live in peace, and let tranquillity always reign in our hearts. It is our part diligently to cultivate our souls, and therefore we must faithfully attend to it; but, as for the abundance of the crop or harvest, let us leave that in our Lord's hands. The husbandman will never be reprehended for not having a good harvest, but only if he did not carefully till and sow his ground.

That is from the *Treatise on the Love of God,* which might be called the advanced course in the curriculum of St.

Francis. I recommend also his *Introduction to the Devout Life,* which he wrote for two laywomen in France but which has enduring virtue for clergy in America.

George Herbert has come into his own recently in our departments of English, as a prince among the "metaphysical poets." Not yet has he recovered an equal place within his own clerical brotherhood. The Wesleys knew him well, and gave him position second only to themselves in that first American hymnal which they issued at Charleston, South Carolina. Only two of Herbert's poems survive in the current *Methodist Hymnal,* and the same two in the Episcopal. One of these appears in the Presbyterian book, and the other in the Congregational. It is high time for us to catch up with the literary crowd, and to go beyond them in seeing not only the poet's verbal artistry but also his unpretentious piety. I shall take the space here for only two lines and a half:

> Dress and undress thy soul; mark the decay
> And growth of it; if, with thy watch, that too
> Be down, then wind up both.

Much that Sir Thomas Browne knew of medicine in the reign of the first Charles has proved now not to be so, and much that he never dreamed of in his profession has been securely learned. The religious faith that he held, not being rooted in the things of the flesh, has suffered less of subtraction and addition in the passing years. In the same vein as St. John and St. Francis, the doctor observes:

I can hardly think there was ever any scared into Heaven; they go the fairest way to Heaven that would serve God without a Hell; other Mercenaries, that crouch into him in fear of Hell, though they term themselves the servants, are indeed but the slaves, of the Almighty;

and thus also in Browne's prayer, "Dispose of me according to the wisdom of thy pleasure: thy will be done, though in my own undoing."

Across the channel in France, Blaise Pascal invented a calculating machine at age eighteen. At age thirty-four he discovered God in Christ Jesus. Mathematicians and physicists still build on his triangle and on his law of pressure. Christians ever may learn from this scientist's direct apprehension of God and his perceptive counsel to men. The opening lines of the *Thoughts* of Pascal well might have been written of many an earthbound scientist of today: "Let them at least learn what is this religion that they assail, before they assail it." And when you and I find intellectual doubting in ourselves, we need to be reminded that "God wishes rather to influence the will than the mind. Perfect clearness would serve the mind and injure the will." There is then peace for us in the realization that "Nothing but the truth gives assurance. Nothing but the sincere search after truth gives rest."

Pastor Luther was not the only influence on the Reverend Mr. Wesley on 24 May 1738. Earlier that afternoon Wesley had attended Evensong at St. Paul's, and had been deeply stirred by the chanting of Psalm 130, the *De profundis*. Earlier still, and for much longer, he had been feeding his spirit on Jeremy Taylor and William Law, the latter of whom still was living at King's Cliffe in Northamptonshire. Bishop Taylor, a royalist who was chaplain to Charles I, and for some time a prisoner under the Commonwealth, was raised to the see of Down and Connor at the Restoration. While he was under official disfavor he wrote *The Rule and Exercise of Holy Living* in 1650, and followed it with *The Rule and Exercise of Holy Dying* in 1651.

What did the eager young Fellow of Lincoln College find

in these works of the long-ago Fellow of All Souls? He found, to begin with, three general "Instruments of Holy Living." These were "Care of our Time," "Purity of Intention," and "The Practice of the Presence of God." He found long chapters on "Christian Sobriety," "Christian Justice," and "Christian Religion." Under this last he read sixteen "Rules for the Practice of Prayer," of which the first is that "We must be careful that we never ask any thing of God that is sinful," and the last enjoins prayer "as a solemn duty morning and evening," but also adjures that we "fail not to make opportunities to worship God at some other times of the day."

Any talk of death is unfashionable in these days of "slumber rooms" and pastel mortuary chapels. Our fashion is less than Christian, for the realism of the Christian faith will not try to hide the final fact of this our earthly life. "Remember that thou art under a supervening necessity," writes this Christian realist. "Nothing is intolerable that is necessary." The same realism points out that "confidence hath destroyed many souls, and many have had a sad portion who have reckoned themselves in the calendar of saints." The conclusion is inevitable:

That we who are alive should so live, and by the actions of religion attend the coming of the day of the Lord, that we neither be surprised nor leave our duties imperfect, nor our sins uncanceled, nor our persons unreconciled, nor God unappeased.

Wesley had Bishop Taylor on his bookshelf. We need him too on ours, and we shall profit by taking him off the shelf often and reading him with self-scrutinizing care.

Said the skeptic historian Edward Gibbon of the pietist hermit William Law, "He left the reputation of a worthy and a pious man, who believed all that he professed and practised all that he enjoined." *A Serious Call to a Devout and Holy Life* was published in 1729, and almost immediately John and Charles Wesley began to visit and consult with its author. Law was pious and simple indeed, but he was not lacking in pungency. How shrewdly he portrays so many laymen of our own day, and not a few college professors:

The one only thing which has not fallen under his improvement, nor receiv'd any benefit from his judicious mind, is his devotion: This is just in the same poor state it was, when he was only six years of age; and the old man prays now, in that little form of words which his mother us'd to hear him repeat night and morning.

Once more the menace of a commercial, reward-and-punishment ethic is sharply pointed out:

We wonder to see grown men acted and govern'd by ambition, envy, scorn, and a desire of glory; not considering that they were all the time of their youth call'd upon to all their action and industry upon the same principle.

Here is the summation of the matter, as Law sees it:

Courage and bravery are words of a great sound, and seem to signify an heroick spirit; but yet humility, which seems to be the lowest, meanest part of devotion, is a more certain argument of a noble and courageous mind. For humility contends with greater enemies, is more constantly engaged, more violently assaulted, bears more, suffers more, and requires greater courage to support itself, than any instances of worldly bravery. . . .

All worldly attainments, whether of greatness, wisdom or bravery, are but empty sounds; and . . . there is nothing wise, or great, or noble, in an human spirit, but rightly to know, and heartily worship and adore the great God, that is the support and life of all spirits, whether in heaven or on earth.

I have been quoting a great deal, yet only the tiniest fragments from a vaster treasury than any one of us can run his fingers through. The fault of this brief selecting is the fault also of the devotional anthologies: not that they fail to reproduce, if they are honestly done, but that they can not reproduce enough. The proper service of the anthology is that it should remind us of sources we have neglected, and introduce us perhaps to some we have not known. Beyond that the responsibility is ours, to do our own searching and to make our own discoveries.

Two areas of specific devotional resource I have left unmentioned hitherto, and shall not attempt to discuss beyond the naming of them. One is the literature of religious traditions other than the Hebrew-Christian. It will help us to know the Greek plays, with their searching analysis of human necessity under inscrutable divine power.—No, I shall not leave out Euripides, as paraphrased by Gilbert Murray:

> What else is Wisdom? What of man's endeavour
>   Or God's high grace so lovely and so great?
>   To stand from fear set free, to breathe and wait;
>   To hold a hand uplifted over Hate;
> And shall not Loveliness be loved for ever?

Classical philosophy has its religious overtones not only in Plato, but very definitely in the Stoic Emperor Marcus Aurelius and the Stoic slave Epictetus, and scarcely less, if more surprisingly, in the *De rerum natura* of the Epicurean poet Lucretius. We shall profit by seeing the conflict of light and darkness in the Zoroastrian *Zend-Avesta,* and the struggle between desire and duty in the Hindu *Bhagavad-Gita.* Buddhist quietism and Confucian empiricism have lessons to teach us too, and so has the stirring faith of the *Quran,* especially in the earlier of the prophet's revelations.

The other body of devotional writing, one which I confess means less to me than those which I have been discussing, is the vast bulk of the materials that belong to our own time. One obvious fact about this is that much of it is highly derivative, and precisely from the older classics of the consecrated life. A further question arises, though from no fault of the modern authors' own: namely, that these new works have not been tested in the crucible of time, and that therefore no one can gauge precisely their survival value. I still am grateful for much of inspiration gained in my younger days from Harry Emerson Fosdick and E. Stanley Jones, and I still have them on my shelves; but I admit that I don't pull them down very often, and that I didn't think of doing so when I was assembling what I thought to be the essentials for this lecture.

A later day may adjudge me mistaken on this point. I am persuaded, however, that no day will confute an affirmative evaluation of St. Augustine and Thomas à Kempis, and Herbert and Browne, and Taylor and Law. These which I have mentioned, along with the holy Scriptures, have fed the souls of men in many an age and in every sort of circumstance. They will feed us too, in so far as we adopt them into our spiritual diet, to the building of sturdy souls and the inspiring of triumphant spirits.

The Content of Devotion

It has not been by ex parte selection, but by the inevitable quality of the truly dedicated life, that so much of what I have quoted turns out to bear upon a single point. The Old Testament phrasing of it is in that inspired mistranslation in the book of Job: "Though he slay me, yet will I trust him." In the New Testament it appears in Jesus' "To sit on my right hand, or on my left, is not mine to give." The *Bhagavad-Gita* sums it up in the couplet,

> Thy business is with deeds alone,
> Not with the fruits the deeds may yield.

The essence of devout, devoted living is that it gives no consideration to the measuring of results, external or even inward. "Trust in God, and do the right," was written (as one would expect) by a Calvinistic Scot; but it expresses the obligation of every Christian all of the time. "Not for weight of glory, not for crown or palm," have we enlisted in the army of our Lord. We may lose every battle on earth, and we have no merit whereby we may claim for ourselves a seat in heaven. That will be given to those for whom it is prepared.

We still are called to fight the good fight, whatever be the visible outcome or the apparent prospect. We still are required to find the Lord's way for us, as best we may, and then to follow it as faithfully as under God we can. No counting of the score is relevant, and any such counting betrays a fissure in our faith. To commit ourselves totally to our God, to ask for no repayment and to think of none, to serve the right because it is the right and we are its servants: this is the duty of every Christian, and this marks with merciless intensity the character of the Christian minister. How shall we stay in character? Only by devoting ourselves wholly to our eternal God, only by surrendering ourselves totally to the fulfillment of his will in us.

This is where "pray without ceasing" fits in, and where it becomes a prime essential. Our devotions are not, may not be, can not be limited to the minutes on rising and retiring, nor to the daily half-hour before the altar. The devotional life is the whole life, or it is no devotion at all. It gains strength from the past, that it may pour out that strength in the present. It draws upon the treasury of God's grace, and it expends all upon the doing of God's will. It retires to the secret place in order that it may appear, unsullied and unfrightened, before all the world.

Our ministry knows no cleavage between the cloistered order and the preaching one. Here we have been thinking chiefly of the cloister. That we need to do, there we need to be, for the voice of God speaks to us with less of interruption when there is nothing else that we can hear. But what the voice of God says to us is, "Go and be my messenger." It is no less an act of religion to befriend a sinner than to reverence a saint, no less a devotion to contend against an injustice than to say a prayer.

This final inquiry ends therefore where the whole series began: with the proposition that twenty-four hours a day, seven days a week, fifty-two weeks in every year, constitute the minimum time for the man of God to persist in that character. He will need a central peace, subsisting at the heart of the world's endless agitation. He can find specific, disciplined means toward the securing of that peace. It is in the agitation, nevertheless, not apart from it, that his peace of mind will be the veritable peace of God. In that peace he will face the world and yet he will be himself, his heart untroubled because nothing can make him afraid.

We have vowed to our God our devotion in the absolute. That devotion is one, alike behind the scenes and before the curtain. Actors we are, but our acting for God is our life's full reality.

EPILOGUE

Last summer a student quoted to me from a letter which her brother had received from their mother. The boy was about to enter his last undergraduate year in college, and had not made up his mind about a career. "Why not go into the Church?" his mother had written him. "The work is easy, the social status is good, and you don't really have to believe in God."

The boy is not going into the Church, and he was as annoyed at the letter as I was. I can not think that many men are dishonest enough, or silly enough, to enter the ministry for motives such as these; and may God forgive any parson who gave to that woman the impression of clerical laziness and duplicity which she seems to have gained.

Any minister who is not a fool or a knave knew his work would be tough; he didn't care about social status, and he believed in God—and still does. The witness to that is that he hasn't given up, hasn't retreated into the ease and social acceptability of a business job with a five-day week at hours 9 to 5 (with two hours for lunch, and time off for golf). Our assignment is a rugged one, and it offers little in the way of visible recompense.

It yet is our assignment, and it is one we shall fulfill according to the measure in which we keep the faith in full fidelity. We have been examining some of the background aspects of that fulfillment. Study, curiosity, relaxation, self-discipline, devotion: these are among the requirements. As behind the scenes we persist in these, we may hope to render service publicly among our people and for our God. Backstage and out front, it is ours by God's grace to be not slothful in business, fervent in spirit, serving the Lord.

*　　*　　*

O LORD, support us all the day long of this mortal life, until the shadows lengthen and the evening comes, and the busy world is hushed, and the fever of life is over, and our work is done. Then in thy mercy grant us a safe lodging, and a holy rest, and peace at the last. Amen.
　　　　　　　—John Henry Newman, A.D. 1842–1843.

APPENDIX:

Some Findings of a Questionnaire

The first step in the preparation of these lectures was the sending of a questionnaire to ministers in northern California towns of under 40,000 population. The mailing was graciously done by the office personnel of the Northern California–Nevada Council of Churches, with the kind permission of the Reverend Dr. Abbott Book, Executive Secretary. Below are summaries of the replies to those questions which, when the returns were examined, seemed to have any measure of significance.

* * *

Population of towns: range 350–17,500; median 7,000; average 6,324.

Membership of churches: range 48–875; median 200; average 272.

Denominations, in order of representation: Methodist, Presbyterian, Disciples, Nazarene, Episcopal, Friends, Federated, Seventh Day Adventist, Assemblies of God, Congregational, Lutheran, American Baptist, United Brethren.

Age of ministers: range 22–68; median and average 45.

Education: 89% college graduates; 80% seminary graduates.

94% are married; 80% have children; average number of children 2.42.

Annual income: range $2,400–$6,360; median $4,000; average $3,953.

94% practice family worship, 100% private devotions; average time of family worship, 13 minutes daily (range 5 minutes to 1 hour); of private devotions, 32 minutes daily (range 5 minutes to 2 hours).

Materials most commonly used in family worship: Bible, *Upper Room, Secret Place*. Materials considered "most helpful" in individual devotional life: Bible, *Imitation of Christ*, writings of E. Stanley Jones, *Book of Common Prayer, Upper Room, Book of Worship* (Methodist).

Places of private devotions (not mutually exclusive): home 43%; office 74%; church proper 29%; out of doors 11%; 37% often attend services at other churches, as members of the congregation.

Weekly time devoted to direct sermon preparation: range 2–20 hours; median 10; average 9.5.

Weekly time devoted to preparation for service(s) of worship: range 0–6 hours (8% none); median 2 hours; average 1.75.

44% write out sermons in full, 25% prayers; 92% choose the hymns; 72% do their own typing.

Number of books in personal libraries: range 50–2,000; median 450; average 526. Percentage of these not specifically "religious": range 0–90%; median 20%; average 29%.

44% belong to book clubs in the religious field; 6% to "secular" clubs; an additional 14% have belonged to religious book clubs in the past.

Use of public library: frequent, 43%; occasional, 8%; little or none, 49%.

Average hours weekly spent in reading the Bible, 3.5; other early Christian writings, 1.25 (44% none); devotional classics, 1 (58% none); current religious books, 3.25 (6% none); current "secular" non-fiction, 2 (20% none); current fiction, .75 (64% none); "whodunits" and science fiction, negligible (94% none); poetry, .25 (58% none); religious periodicals, 2.5 (3% none); secular periodicals, 1.25 (33% none); newspapers, 2.25 (6% none). Average total reading time, weekly: 19 hours.

Periodicals taken: range 0–10; median 5; average 5. Religious periodicals most commonly taken: *Christian Advocate, Christian Century, Christian Century Pulpit, Pastoral Psychology, Presbyterian Life, Shepherd, Christian Herald, Church Management.* Secular periodicals most commonly taken: *Reader's Digest, Life, Saturday Evening Post, National Geographic, Time, Atlantic Monthly.* Average number of periodicals read throughout, 1.3; selectively, 2.2; casually, .7.

Principal hobbies: gardening, photography, woodworking, golf, fishing. Principal active sports: fishing, golf, swimming, walking, hunting, tennis. Principal spectator sports: football, baseball, basketball.

69% attend movies, from twice a year to once a week (average 7 times yearly). 69% attend concerts, from once a year to once a week (average 3 times yearly). 44% attend the theater, from once in three years to twice a month (average once yearly).

22% belong to luncheon clubs, 28% to other clubs, 31% to lodges.

53% take a weekly "day off," with Monday the most popular. 93% take an annual vacation; average duration 2 weeks, 5 days.